THE
CONVERSATION IN
HEAVEN

Living Life's Ups & Downs Through Heaven's Lens

ABIGAIL HOLT-JENNINGS
FOREWORD BY JENN STOCKMAN

The Conversation In Heaven:
Living Life's Ups & Downs Through Heaven's Lens

Edited By: David Teems

The Scriptures used in this book are noted as follows:

ISBN 10: 1727396111
ISBN 13: 978-1727396119

# Endorsements

Abigail is a sign and a wonder. Her life is a testimony of God's goodness and grace. In journeying through the story of her life, hearing the conversation in heaven during her trials and victories, you will begin to hear echoes of what heaven has been saying over your own story.

I feel the grace to grow in hope and joy whenever Abigail walks into the room, and I have felt the same grace on every page of this book. Let heaven begin to set the standard of your everyday life.

Blake K. Healy

Director, BASSM (Bethel Atlanta School of Supernatural Ministry)
Author of *The Veil* (Charisma House, 2018)

I have read and fully endorse Abigail's book. Having known Abigail for years, I can say with enthusiasm that she is "real" in every way. Her passion is Christ-given and continually spreads like a rushing, mighty wind. It is evident in her book that she is uniquely gifted with a powerful, creative mind that partners with intellectual brilliance.

Since 1994, I've taught hundreds of graduate students in clinical mental health courses. Having Abigail as a student, reading her book and having talked and walked with her through many of the life experiences you will read about on these pages, I can truly say that she has an extraordinary ability to integrate the Gospel with victory and loss in ways that brings forth life and healing to others.

My unequivocal, scientific conclusion is that God is real, Jesus is alive, and the Holy Spirit continually reaches out to help us.

Abigail's book is a gift of hope and healing to all people. Each page exhibits her contagious, energetic personality and demands focus and attention to the subject - the life healing work of Jesus Christ.

Perhaps her book's greatest contribution is the legacy that it brings to her children, River and Lily. I have long seen her unique wisdom and giftedness encompassed in her son River and Abigail's love for people in her daughter, Lily Grace.

This book will undoubtedly remain forever stamped upon their hearts, minds and many future families.

Abigail is one of life's great blessings. I appreciate very much that she has written this book. Its inspiration is of such that I plan to read it several more times and use it as a textbook resource for students at the graduate school.

Dr. Luke Queen

MBA, M.Ed., M.Div, D.Min., LPC-MHSP, MAC, NCGC, NCC (Board Certified)

Clinical Faculty & Supervision at
The Pentecostal Theological Seminary

Regional Vice President & Executive Compliance Officer
Evergreen Life Services

Licensed Mental Health Consultant
Recovery Court (Adolescent & Adult) Mental Health Court
Chattanooga, TN

This book chronicles Abigail's journey taking on Goliath and a few of his brothers. She joined the fight as only she can: brave, bold and beautiful. We've watched her gracefully navigate the maze of the medical community, alternative medicine and her faith in the Healer. On the difficult and scary days, she drew on her inner circle, including our entire community in her victory celebration.

Turn the diamond in the light and you see a different reflection. Don't try to put Abigail in a box or category. At times she's bold. Other times, she's a sensitive, professional counselor. She's a scholar but can stand on a stump and preach Pentecost with fire! She'll shovel the barn by day and be the "belle of the ball" by night. She's the beauty around town and the beast in the gym. She's a mom and a minister. She's the healer and the healed.

The Conversation in Heaven is a story for today – a story of navigating medicine and healing, calling on family and community, and seeing the miracle working God in our midst! Feel yourself going deeper, wider and higher in your own faith journey with every page!

Steve & Lindy Hale
Senior Leaders, Bethel Atlanta Church

We have known Abigail for the past twenty-five years, as a youth leader and an amazing friend-for-life. She has been more like a sister to my wife and me, but to my children, she is and will always be "Aunt Abigail."

Abigail's life has been one of passion; passion for God, family, friends and life. Her passion is fueled by her purpose; a purpose much bigger than herself. She lives life to the full, at about 120%, if that's even possible and her cup of joy runs over as her love and laughter fills the room.

Behind the laughter and zest for life is a woman who is deeply in love with Jesus Christ and has experienced an intimacy with her Heavenly Father that few experience except through the fellowship of suffering.

Behind the beauty pageant queen, is a real person who has walked through "the valley of the shadow of death" as she battled cancer and nearly lost her life. It is through this horrific battle that she experienced a life-giving conversation in heaven that has transformed her life and now, you and I get to eavesdrop on that conversation.

Today, Abigail is cancer-free, but she bares the battle scars of a person who has suffered greatly yet has overcome supernaturally through the grace and strength of her Heavenly Father.

I couldn't be prouder or more inspired by Abigail's life and her brave and courageous story of triumph. She is truly one of God's greatest and a real faith-hero, whose name could easily have been placed in Hebrews 11.

May you be inspired to live your life fully alive as Abigail's story encourages and strengthens you to lean into your Heavenly Father as you fight your own life-changing battles.

May you determine to come out stronger and better, testifying to the world of God's amazing grace!

Bill & Jenny McIntosh
Lead Pastors, New Life Church, Farmville, VA

If there is a word that defines Abigail Holt-Jennings, it is the word "effervescence." Each page of her new book pulses with it. Miracles can do that. Being given another chance at life can do that. It can't be helped. Hers is not an easy story to tell, which makes the telling all the more beautiful as it bubbles to the surface. This is a first book, and I am certain as you read and engage with the Abigail I have come to know, as you allow her to instruct, encourage, and cheer you on, you will, with great joy and expectation, anticipate the second, third, and all the books to come.

David Teems
Author of *Tyndale: The Man Who Gave God an English Voice*
(Thomas Nelson/Harper Collins, 2012)
and *Godspeed: Voices of the Reformation*
(Abingdon Press, 2017)

We all walk through the valley as we journey through life. We are defined through our challenges, through our choices, through the opportunities we are given, through the blessings we receive and through the blessings we share with others. The walk that Abigail has gone through has enlightened her with knowledge, with passion, and with a great desire to share, inspire and lift up others. May her story be a blessing to you as it is to so many of us.

Dave Hall
Founder of Cellercise.com and Inventor of *The Cellerciser*

The Conversation In Heaven

Acknowledgements

To my First & Last, my Beginning & my End,
my Forever & my Always, I entirely love you, my Father,
my wonderful Jesus, and my brilliant Holy Spirit.

I want to say a huge thank you to everyone who made this book a reality. Thank you for loving me and believing in the message within these pages through all your countless hours of hard work, designing, brainstorming, editing, valuable feedback and so much more. I am forever grateful for each of you.

My deepest gratitude to David Teems. How was I so blessed to hit the lottery with the best editor ever? You and your wife, Benita, are a delightful surprise gift in my life from Heaven. Thank you for generously sharing your brilliance with me and thank you Laura Lee Douglass, for being "Anna in the temple," seeing full-grown oaks out of acorns.

To my dear, dear friends and forever family at Bethel Atlanta Church and my much-loved pastors and eternal friends, Steve and Lindy Hale. Your obedience and sacrifice to plant a church and ministry school has forever impacted my life and so many others, continuing to multiply the Kingdom forever.

To my "mom friends" and "besties." You all know who you are. All the words in the world couldn't adequately express my heartfelt thankfulness for your friendship, prayers, love, kindness, generosity, self-sacrifice, countless meals, loving me and Jesus well by caring for farm animals, making grocery runs, hospital visits, round-the-clock care, and endless support. On top of all the beautiful ways you loved and supported me, you "kept me alive" with the best gift of all—endless laughter!

To John and Joanne Lee and my entire KONOS family, thank you for your loving friendship and generous support toward the kids and me. You look just like our wonderful Jesus.

To my sweet Gina, thank you for being a hero of Hope, an example I could steady my gaze on, while in the heat of the battle. You are a beautiful champion.

To Dr. Christopher Saxon at *Saxon Health*, I will NEVER forget coming to see you for the first time after being told I had terminal cancer and should begin conventional chemotherapy and radiation right away. You looked right at me and said, "You're not going anywhere." Thank you for being one of the biggest voices of HOPE and healing to me. I am forever grateful for the sacrifices you have made to devote your life to natural healing and never changing that subject. The entire world needs you, my dear friend!

To the best breast surgeon ever, Dr. Nicole Sroka. I feel so blessed that Heaven hand-picked you for me.

To my oncologist, Dr. Trevor Feinstein, thank you for acknowledging, "it didn't take your medical degree on the wall to see that this is a miracle."

To the one whom my soul loves, Jennifer Dawn Stockman, you are forever a dream come true; my treasured "Fridsy" for all time.

To my Mom, your legacy of prayer and intimacy with our Father is forever imprinted on my heart. I love you.

All of you here, carry the ever-beautiful sound of Hope! You are the gorgeous expression of Psalm 126 in my life:

When the Lord restored the fortunes of Zion, we were like those who dream. We laughed and laughed and overflowed with gladness. We were left shouting for joy and singing Your praise. All the nations saw it and joined in, saying, "The Lord has done great miracles for them!" Yes, He did mighty miracles and we are overjoyed! Now, Lord, do it again! Restore us to our former glory! May streams of Your refreshing flow over us until our dry hearts are drenched again. Those who sow their tears as seeds will reap a harvest with joyful shouts of glee. They may weep as they go out carrying their seed to sow, but they will return with joyful laughter and shouting with gladness as they bring back armloads of blessing and a harvest overflowing! (TPT)

The Conversation In Heaven

 Dedication

This book is dedicated to my children,

River Joshua and Lily Grace.

You are born champions, my greatest joys and my most favorite, precious people in this whole, wide, wonderful world.

The Conversation In Heaven

Contents

Foreword 1

1: Never Make Another Penny 5

2: Painted In Blood...Signed: *Jesus* 13

3: Don't Ever Plead My Blood Again 19

4: Jesus Had Stinky Feet 27

5: An Invitation Into The Fellowship of His Sufferings 35

6: Keep Hope Alive by Scrubbing a Bathtub 45

7: Heaven's Waiting Room 55

8: Build Me An Altar 69

9: Surround Yourself with People Who Can See Your Army 81

10: Jesus Likes Watching the Olympics 87

11: Be Sure and Bring a Basket To Your Valley 91

12: When Fear Comes Knocking, Answer the Door! 97

13: When *I* Got Up, *You* Got Up 103

Resources 113

The Conversation In Heaven

 Foreword

There are moments in life when we form relationships with people because of our own intention to know and be known by them. Then, there are those moments in life when we bump into people along the path of a shared and single pursuit to relentlessly give our lives to seek first His Kingdom. We look over through the blood, sweat, and tears and find a covenant friend is running with all her might in the same direction towards His face. We find we are better, stronger, and burning brighter because she is running by our side. A friend who pulls us in to a greater awareness and deeper gaze on the person of Jesus is a friend we will cherish for the rest of time.

Abigail is one of those friends. Her lens is full of the thing Paul strained forward and pressed on for in Philippians 3, *"to know Him."* She has truly counted it all as loss, trash on a garbage heap, to be intimately acquainted with the power of His resurrection and the invitation in His suffering.

I have had the honor of doing life beside her—worshipping with unreserved passion, homeschooling our children, holding hands in hospital beds, laughing until we can't breathe—through life's ups and downs, her lens remains full of a Jesus, Who is worth it.

I have been wildly impacted by the way she sees from Heaven's eternal perspective, and as you read the pages of this book, you will be too.

Abigail is a sign and a wonder that points to an open door to enter into the more of His Presence. Ephesians 2:7 says, *"Throughout the coming ages we will be the visible display of the infinite, limitless riches of His grace and kindness, which was showered upon us in Jesus Christ"* - (TPT).

She is this visible display, a living invitation, to whole-heartedly abandon ourselves to the one conversation worth giving our lives to. *The Conversation In Heaven* is full of profound revelation and stunning stories of His grace and kindness that will leave your heart absolutely undone. The most moving part of this book, though, is His Presence that rests on the words.

Abigail's history with God is woven through every chapter, taking us deeper into the conversation in Heaven over our own.

I will never forget the day I sat beside Abigail as the doctor went over the cancer report you will hear about in this book. I don't really remember much of the conversation that took place on earth but what's seared into my memory was the moment I realized that we were in the enemy's camp. For generations cancer had come to steal, kill, and destroy throughout the family line of my dear, most cherished friend. The enemy thought we were in his camp that day to continue the conversation he was having, but, he was wrong. We were only in that camp to watch a warrior, hero, and friend of God plunder and take back all that had been stolen.

Heroes are the ones who step into the dark space as a yielded vessel, to let God write His story. Abigail's children's children will not shudder when they hear the word "cancer." Instead, they will celebrate and see through the lens of Heaven that cancer is a defeated foe, a chewed-up piece of gum under the victorious foot of Jesus! The enemy will be the one eternally shuddering at the sound of her legacy coming his way.

What is taunting your family line? Cancer? Divorce? Fear? As you listen to the conversation in Heaven about you, you will find, that you too, are a warrior, hero and friend of God. I'm certain as you read this book, you will find yourself stepping into the dark space to be the yielded vessel that whole-heartedly trusts in the One Who is worth it. On the other side of the darkness you will find yourself sitting in the bright victory of Jesus, like Abigail and generations of heroes who've *"staggered out of the tomb, awestruck, with their minds swirling"*
- Mark 16:8 (TPT).

Jenn Stockman
First Year Director, BASSM (Bethel Atlanta School of Supernatural Ministry)
Author of The War on Your Voice (2018)

The Conversation In Heaven

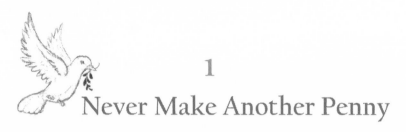

1
Never Make Another Penny

I might as well begin this book from present day and track back upon the beautiful timeline of my life. Though many would not describe it as beautiful, Heaven does.

I am a single Mom with two amazing children—a brilliant and extremely witty fourteen-year-old son named River Joshua and a fascinating and fully alive, twelve-year-old songbird of a daughter, Lily Grace. I homeschool my children, earned a master's degree in mental health, marriage and family counseling, am an exercise and wellness trainer, founded a cool fitness rebounding company called Jumpology, and I am a counselor and 2nd year ministry school revival pastor at the Bethel Atlanta School of Supernatural Ministry (BASSM), just outside of Atlanta, Georgia.

We have a fabulous, fat pig named Wilb*her* (we thought "she" was a "he" until recently), seven fluffy, egg-laying chickens, two cats, one talkative parrot, and one extremely loved and spoiled goldendoodle named Luey.

I have loved the Lord for as long as I can remember and want to know no other life than the one fully lived in Him. I am hearing and following His Voice in writing this book and feel delightfully frozen in my tracks until I do so.

I don't know about you, but I have spent too many of my years working need-oriented jobs instead of living by His Voice. Recently, a few, dear friends of mine and I got together just to be with Him and each other. As we were praying, laughing and hanging out, I heard the Father say to me, "I never want you to make another penny out of need, only out of purpose."

This one statement from Him completely changed my income lens. On top of my other jobs, I most recently relinquished a great job as a personal trainer at the swanky, country club here in town. I came and went as I pleased, made my own schedule, chose my own clients, but I knew deep, deep down it was not my purpose, and, while a great opportunity, I felt worn out by having added it to my plate. You see, I took it out of need.

Not the kind of need that is healthy and realistic but the kind of need that has its roots in fear, not faith. The kind of need that is driven by lack, striving, anxiety and fear. The kind that causes us to jump at any opportunity that comes our way and answer the loudest voice we hear, not the One we know in the deepest part of our hearts is His.

That voice of need will burn you out, zap your energy, steal your creativity and stifle your imagination. The dreamer in you doesn't get a voice or any property of your own in that land of need, therefore, nothing of any substance or eternal value can be built there. No soil exists in Heaven made of need nor can any fruit be cultivated there.

Need looks like Adam forgetting his identity as a son and listening to another tell him who he was, sacrificing his destiny on that oh, so needy altar of compromise.

Need looks like Abraham and Sarah, listening to its loud voice by interfering with Heaven's faith-filled voice of purpose. A voice with no need to shout, a voice that carries the tone of patience and faithfully waits, waits for a destined son of promise named Isaac. Promise housed in purpose, birthed through impossibility and germinated in the soil of faith, a soil found in the expired womb of Sarah. Their clear vision of faith-filled purpose, was temporarily traded for the foggy lenses of need as they took their maidservant Hagar and birthed a needy counterfeit named Ishmael, creating a difficult and costly mess for the nation of Israel.

Need looks like King Saul disobeying the voice of the prophet Samuel and forfeiting his right to the throne, yet true to His nature, God redeems it all through His servant David.

Aaah, but purpose! You see, your purpose will bring an unending energy with it, the fuel of Heaven to be exact, which I believe, is the truest definition of passion. Purpose has its foundations and almost requirements in the land that "doesn't make sense." The land filled with cliff edges, huge risks, apparent failures, and seemingly, sure defeats. This is often the most beautiful breeding ground for purpose to flourish. In the Kingdom, we call purpose the land of faith, for it is in this land where we find pleasing God to be so satisfying.

> *And without faith living within us it would be impossible to please God. For we come to God in faith knowing that He is real and that He rewards the faith of those who give all their passion and strength into seeking Him.*
> *- Hebrews 11:6 (TPT)*

Purpose looks like God telling Noah to build a boat when no one even knew what rain was. Yet through his obedience, passion-filled purpose fueled every swing of his hammer throughout the almost seventy-ish years it took to build that purpose-driven boat, saving his entire family and mankind, putting God's eternal covenant on display, and preserving our much-loved creeping species of all kinds.

Purpose looks like God calling Mary to grow His Son in her body, making no sense to anyone around her. Yet from the angel's first visit, her heart was fueled by an eternal passion that was captivated with her obedient yes to purpose, altering eternity for you and me.

Purpose looks like Daniel's unrelenting heart of obedience to continue praying to His beloved God and living a life of uncompromising integrity, despite the world's standards around him. That purpose was backed by all of Heaven as even violent mouths of lions had to bow their insatiable appetites to a man that would have been their lunch, bow to a purpose that would save a king and a nation; a purpose in whose writings and revelations we still glean from today.

Now, let me just say what we do need. We need each other. It's very important that you surround yourself with like-minded believers who can hear with you, for you, and, at times, in spite of you. There are things the Lord will certainly show us by ourselves, in intimate times and places with Him that only belong to you and Him but then there are other things He wants to show you through and only through another. Pay close attention not to isolate yourself from the Body (fear, shame and guilt usually are the culprits of this kind of isolation but more on this later). Never judge the voice or vessel He may speak through to reach you. I think He likes to do that to keep us guessing. After all, He is God and reserves the right to His own mystique. Furthermore, it creates opportunity for us to live humbly and reliant to receive from Him and one another, no matter what the delivery package may look like.

So, back to what He said. That's right, as I'm writing this book, it was just recently that He spoke these words to my heart. After making so many mistakes in trying to obey Him yet adding my own efforts to the pot, I have learned that whole-hearted obedience is the only kind that reaps full and eternal rewards, pleasing the heart of God like nothing else.

For me, when my own brains and reasoning get involved, a recipe for disaster ensues. The sooner we decide to go ahead and lose our minds to gain His, the better. Take it from me and my mountain of mistakes in this area and grab the shortcut of wisdom and experience I am offering you to a successful, happy life. What is that shortcut? Pure, unadulterated obedience to God. Plain and simple, right? Well, the world's way of doing things would say "wrong" but there again, if you just go ahead and surrender to the truth that you are to be in this world but not of it (in your thinking and decision-making), you will bypass many a heartache, my friend. The last time I checked, the Lord really isn't in to duplex living, He'd rather take up residence in a single dwelling.

I have given them Your message and that is why the unbelieving world hates them. For their allegiance is no longer to this world because I am not of this world. I am not asking that You remove them from the world, but I ask that You guard their hearts from evil, for they no longer belong to this world any more than I do. Your Word is truth! So, make them holy by the truth.

- John 17:14-17 (TPT)

His Voice, the Voice of truth, will be the greatest Truth you will ever want and need to know. Throw understanding and rationale out the window. Just ". . . trust and obey, for there's no other way, to be happy in Jesus but to trust and obey." Isn't that a song somewhere?

On top of that lidless trust, release yourself into wild obedience and surrender to His Voice found within these words of truth:

For we did not receive the spirit of this world system but the Spirit of God, so that we might come to understand and experience all that grace has lavished upon us. And we articulate these realities with the words imparted to us by the Spirit and not with the words taught by human wisdom. We join together Spirit-revealed truths with Spirit-revealed words. Someone living on an entirely human level rejects the revelations of God's Spirit, for they make no sense to him. He can't understand the revelations of the Spirit because they are only discovered by the illumination of the Spirit. Those who live in the Spirit are able to carefully evaluate all things and they are subject to the scrutiny of no one but God. For who has ever intimately known the mind of the Lord Yahweh well enough to become His counselor? Christ has, and we possess Christ's perceptions. - 1 Corinthians 2:12-16 (TPT)

Giving in to His Voice will be the most adventurous life you will ever know-guaranteed. Stop trying to make or wait for everyone around you to "get it" because, loving news flash-they won't.

Jump on the roller coaster, strap in, and hold on as best you can. Uncompromised obedience to Him will be the most fulfilling yet unknowing, terrifying yet gratifying, wild yet deeply satisfying ride of your life!

The Conversation In Heaven

2

Painted In Blood... Signed: *Jesus*

One of my most favorite things to do is counseling. No matter the size of the degree on my wall or the number of trainings I've completed, no amount of education and knowledge can trump the brilliance of Holy Spirit.

I love to experience the stellar Counselor Himself show up fully in each session and accomplish all that is on Heaven's agenda for that very special son or daughter. I never doubt He will hit a home run and I stay delighted that He puts the ball in my hand and the bat in the hands of a willing and often, fearful, wounded warrior. Yet as we partner with Him, a home run is hit every time.

One day, I was in session with a precious gal. She had driven a long way and was so hungry for God yet struggling in her own identity and failures which caused her connection with God, herself and others to feel disjointed, unfulfilling and inadequate. As we began to talk and process through this, I felt the need to pray.

One thing I love about our church and the Christian culture we belong to is a very powerful tool we use in helping others along their journey to healing, freedom and wholeness. This tool is called Sozo ministry. *Sozo* is the Greek word translated, "saved, delivered and healed."

Sozo ministry is a unique inner healing and deliverance ministry aimed to get to the root of things that may be hindering our personal connection with the Father, Son and Holy Spirit. With a healed connection, you can walk in the destiny to which you have been called.

> *I am the Gateway. To enter through Me is to experience life, freedom and satisfaction. A thief has only one thing in mind—he wants to steal, slaughter and destroy. But I have come to give you everything in abundance, more than you expect—life in its fullness until you overflow!*
> - John 10:9-11 (TPT)

If your life is anything less than abundant in every area, if you are not living in fullness, ask the Father where the deficit is? What lie(s) are you possibly believing that are causing you to live any area of your life in less than all Jesus purchased for you to extravagantly spend and enjoy? What areas do you feel you are coming up "short" in—physically, emotionally and/or spiritually? Heaven is never at a point of lack, insufficiency or deficit, so neither should you be.

> *For He is the complete fullness of Deity living in human form. And our own completeness is now found in Him. We are completely filled with God as Christ's fullness overflows within us.* - Colossians 2:9-10 (TPT)

Back to my gal. As we were praying, I was taken into a vision. She and I, (we'll call her Brittany), were standing in a long hallway in the upstairs part of what looked to be a large, antebellum home. Luxurious, red carpet lined this huge hallway and all along the wall, as far as I could see, were massive paintings, one after the other. As we stepped up to one of the paintings, the scene was from a very vivid event in Brittany's life, definitely an event one would not want to hang anywhere. The scene was filled with guilt, hurt, sin, shame and regret. As we stood there, a bit in disbelief that all of this was hanging up on display, for everyone to see, I could feel Brittany's embarrassment, nakedness, vulnerability and shame.

Suddenly, Jesus walked up to us. He stood there, such peace and calmness on His face, even a slight smile, which conveyed the deepest love one could ever comprehend. He reached up and took His Hand as if it were a paintbrush and began "painting" over the picture. As His Hand painted down the canvas, rich Blood flowed from His fingers, completely covering what was underneath. His Hand would brush all the way to the bottom and start at the top again; over and over until the whole painting was covered in the richest, thickest Blood imaginable, leaving no trace of the horrible scene before.

When the entire painting was covered, He looked over at Brittany. His approving smile and the kindness in His Eyes removed all doubt that He had anything but the greatest love for His daughter. He turned back to the painting, as it dripped in His priceless Blood. With His right index finger, He signed His Name in the right-hand corner, *Jesus.*

What? He made that painting His! How could He do that? He took the most shameful and sinful parts of Brittany's life and redeemed them as His own. Redeemed literally means, "to buy back."

I was undone. She was undone. We were left a puddle of messy tears. Brittany said this moment changed her life forever, knowing she would never be the same.

I knew I wouldn't either.

Oh dear friend, when you invite Jesus in to your messiness, your shame, guilt, your hurt, your pain—He gets right in the middle of it, redeems it and uncovers the lies that have held you captive from fully loving Him, fully loving you, and fully loving others. The voice of shame is silenced, and the voice of freedom is turned up loud and clear.

When you allow Him to "cut the lights on" in every area of your life, the rooms you have locked and bolted shut, the rooms you are terrified of anyone seeing or knowing, those rooms are the ones He wants to fully be in, to entirely decorate with His love, forgiveness, redemption, and restoration.

The old shiplap we now use to remodel that has become so trendy, came from somebody's scrap pile, somebody's trash heap, waiting to be burned or thrown away. God is the greatest Recycler the world will ever know. Heaven wastes nothing. Everything is redeemed, repurposed and yes, put on display with greater value than it was ever thought or seen of having before.

> *Through our union with Him we have experienced circumcision of heart. All of the guilt and power of sin has been cut away and is now extinct because of what Christ, the Anointed One, has accomplished for us. For we've been buried with Him into His death. Our "baptism into death" also means we were raised with Him when we believed in God's resurrection power, the power that raised Him from death's realm. This "realm of death" describes our former state, for we were held in sin's grasp. But now, we've been resurrected out of*

that "realm of death" never to return, for we are forever alive and forgiven of all our sins! He canceled out every legal violation we had on our record and the old arrest warrant that stood to indict us. He erased it all—our sins, our stained soul—He deleted it all and they cannot be retrieved!

Everything we once were in Adam has been placed onto His cross and nailed permanently there as a public display of cancellation. Then Jesus made a public spectacle of all the powers and principalities of darkness, stripping away from them every weapon and all their spiritual authority and power to accuse us. And by the power of the cross, Jesus led them around as prisoners in a procession of triumph. He was not their prisoner; they were His! So why would you allow anyone to judge you...? - Colossians 2:11-16 (TPT)

If you are experiencing any shame or guilt that is hindering you from living your life with every light fully flipped on and shining bright, I encourage you to take a stroll with your Heavenly Father, His Son, Jesus (your big Brother, by the way) and the Holy Spirit. Hard to believe that Jesus is your Brother?

Jesus, the Holy One, makes us holy. And as sons and daughters, we now belong to His same Father, so He is not ashamed or embarrassed to introduce us as His brothers and sisters! - Hebrews 2:11 (TPT)

So yes, walk down that hallway with your Heavenly Father, your big Brother Jesus and the forever brilliant Holy Spirit.

Stop with Them at every painting, every scene that has brought you any pain, shame, or guilt that has been illegally robbing you of living in His fullness.

Watch as your Jesus, the One Who is forever for you, your biggest Fan, permanently paints over every painful scene and signs His beautiful Name in each and every corner. Stay in that hallway until any voice that has been lying to you is silenced once and for all. Choose to be made free to enjoy His fullness in every area of your wonderful, abundantly-filled life.

3
Don't Ever Plead My Blood Again

During my own journey of healing from a devastating divorce, I went through a season of time, all necessary and completely normal, by the way, where I felt so broken and hurt in what seemed to be every possible area of my life.

I have a saying that if you were to cut me open, I bleed family, so going through such an insurmountable loss in this area, was pain that felt excruciating on every level. A pain that was 24/7, every second of every minute of every hour; a pain that never seemed to let up. It hurt to breathe.

Divorce is one of the top three most devastating things that can happen to a human being, so give yourself loads of grace if you're in that boat right now. My husband and I pastored a church together for twelve years. Not only was my marriage bulldozed, our church, community, meaningful relationships, and my reputation were leveled as well.

I love deeply, so it is very understandable that the depth of pain I was experiencing was very, very deep as well. Right in the middle of that, I lost my baby sister to a car accident while she served our country in the Navy. She was my best buddy, my playmate, even my roommate at times. We were only eighteen months apart. We shared everything together—clothes, makeup, sports, even boys. I had the privilege of seeing her blossom so beautifully in her relationship with God.

I didn't understand the levels of pain, loss and grief I was experiencing then, like I do now. I was actually grieving and mourning on the inside at a depth that was so vast, it seemed suffocating. Christ fascinatingly pardoned and even redeemed many mistakes I made during this time of hurt and pain.

The reality was, life continued to go on all around me and suddenly, being a single Mom brought financial demands with it that took no time for grief. However, nothing was going to be right again until I fully faced this season and oddly enough, embraced it.

Oh friend, if you find yourself in a place of great pain, disappointment or loss, take the critical and absolutely required time to mourn and grieve. Jesus Himself said, as He preached His first public sermon, His famous "Sermon on the Mount," in Matthew 5:4, *"Blessed are they who mourn, for they will be comforted"* (ESV). When you can accept your season as a season of mourning, just like we see winter coming and we prepare our houses, cars, grass, plants, etc., you will be able to give yourself permission to embrace it, which will allow you to be comforted in a way that will produce healing, further helping you walk in wholeness and freedom.

Pastor Bill Johnson says three things try to cripple the people of God like nothing else: bitterness, resentment, and disappointment. Being a pastor and counselor for quite some time now, I believe these ugly three are able to take root in our lives when we do not give ourselves the very necessary time to grieve, mourn, and then, forgive; if we don't allow our hearts this critical time, these deadly emotions have a breeding ground to thrive, wreaking havoc in the gardens of our hearts.

Human nature can be fickle, and, sadly, very opinionated at times, having no truth to substantiate those opinions. Many accusations and false judgments were dished out on my plate during this painful season, but I felt the best thing to do was not open my mouth to defend myself. A mentor of mine used to say that if we are to experience deep places in God, we must develop an appetite for the bread of misunderstanding. I ate more loaves than I ever wanted to of that bread.

The Bible is so clear we are to never put our trust in man or their opinions. Love deeply, and yes, have beautiful and meaningful relationships, but don't place unrealistic demands of trust and dependence upon another person that are only reserved in your heart for God and God alone. If others' opinions of you begin to matter, you will constantly be riding a roller coaster with its speed dictated by their approval or disapproval. This, my friend, will be a nauseous and miserable ride.

You may be in a painful season like this right now. If not, I'm almost positive you have someone in your life who is. Pray for endless amounts of grace and understanding because you have no idea that the "King David" you are talking to, may just temporarily be living in their own "cave of Adullam." What's *Adullam*?

Adullam was a royal city where the scene of David's memorable victory over the giant, Goliath, occurred.

However, no memory of a victory is being discussed as David finds himself deep in a cave, King Saul hot on his heels to kill him out of jealousy, his own son trying to snatch the throne while also sleeping with his wives, and his close buddies being men who were in distress, in debt and discontented. Talk about someone not coming across as victorious or glamorous! David may have temporarily forgotten who he was, his own family and friends definitely forgot who he was, but Heaven never changed Its conversation about David.

Interestingly enough, the word Adullam has one of its origins found in the word *hero*. This hero-king was hiding out in a cave with men who were on the lowest rung of society's success ladder; yet his identity as king never changed, even when his season did.

You see, King David was the greatest Old Testament king that Israel would ever know. He was a worshipper and a warrior. As a young boy, he knew how to love, serve, and lead his sheep, qualifying him to later lead many people. Even when he messed up, he was very self-aware about his mistakes, quick to confess and equally as quick to believe and receive God's unending love and forgiveness for himself. He is a gorgeous Old Testament example of our wonderful Jesus and is a great mirror of insight into ourselves, as well.

Oh friends, you never know who you will meet along life's way in their own "cave of Adullam." Be very careful not to judge anyone's season. Seasons, by design, will change. Don't define another by their season and equally important, don't define yourself there, either.

One day, as I was in my own cave of Adullam, walking and talking to the Lord, crying out to Him for what seemed to be the thousandth time to take this crippling pain from me, I began to "plead" the blood of Jesus. It's all I knew to do and all I had been taught to do, growing up in the church. So, like a well-taught church girl, I kept pleading His blood over and over again until He lovingly, yet firmly, interrupted my pleadings with this statement: "Abigail, never plead My blood again. Why would you need to plead for something that is already yours? *Apply*. Apply My blood, Abigail."

Right then I saw a vision of myself walking around like a big piece of Swiss cheese, holes all through me. I looked down and in my left hand, I was holding the handle of a big paint bucket. In my right hand, I carried a paint brush. I peered into the bucket, discovering it was filled to the brim with fresh, rich Blood. I knew right away that it was His Blood and I also knew exactly what to do—apply that Blood to myself and those big, ugly, "Swiss cheese" holes.

I furiously dipped the brush into the bucket and over and over, slathered that rich Blood onto myself. As soon as the Blood touched my "holes," it was like they were sucked up, completely healed and whole, with no evidence of a hole ever being there.

Oh friends, this is the way of our wonderful Jesus! He came to heal our broken hearts, to bind up our wounds, with no stitches or scars to remind us of the previous damage. Psalm 147:3 so beautifully declares, *"He heals the wounds of every shattered heart"* (TPT).

I painted and painted, sloshed and slathered on so much of that Blood, I was sure I had emptied the can. When I looked down to see if there was any more in the bucket I could use, to my amazement, that can of rich and beautiful Blood was still filled to the top; the level had never dropped from its original, full capacity.

I was stunned. I was captivated. In that moment, Heaven began to serenade me:

> . . . *for It reaches to the highest mountains*
> *and it flows to the lowest valleys.*
> *The Blood that gives me strength from day to day,*
> *It will ne-e-ver lose Its power!*

Oh glorious one, there is no pain you may be experiencing too deep, where His blood can't go and flow to heal you, no struggle too great where His Blood can't free you, making you victorious and no mistake or failure too ugly, His Blood can't erase clean, making you completely whole and brand new.

> *He existed before anything was made, and now*
> *everything finds completion in Him... For God is satisfied*
> *to have all His fullness dwelling in Christ. And by the*
> *blood of His cross, everything in Heaven and earth is*
> *brought back to Himself—back to its original intent,*
> *restored to innocence again!*
>
> - Colossians 1:17,19-20 (TPT)

Friend, never again plead for what is already yours. *Apply.*

As equally important is the truth that He came to make us whole. Wholeness is what Jesus purchased and modeled for us. Did you know that all during the Passion of our Christ, His sufferings, the beatings He took for us; in all that suffering, they couldn't break one of His bones? Not one of them was broken. There is so much richness in this truth and just one beautiful part is that Jesus, our Champion Friend, modeled wholeness for us from start to finish.

And the very God of peace sanctify you completely, that your spirit, soul, and body be preserved whole without blame . . . - 1 Thessalonians 5:23 (JUB)

Christ ransomed us at such a huge cost. A cost that bought us entire freedom and complete wholeness. Just as they could not break even one of His bones, not one part of the "bones" of your life has to be lived fragmented or broken.

The Lord is close to all whose hearts are crushed by pain and He is always ready to restore the repentant one. Even when bad things happen to the good and godly ones, the Lord will save them and not let them be defeated by what they face. God will be your bodyguard to protect you when trouble is near. Not one bone will be broken. - Psalm 34:18-20 (TPT)

What would you do if you saw a grown man with a big cast on his leg and a pair of crutches, hobbling up to the starting line of a marathon race, awkwardly trying to squeeze himself next to the other fit and strong runners as he attempted to run that marathon with them? Would you really expect him to be able to do it? How absurd and insensitive would it be if you were mad or frustrated at him because he couldn't?

Well, it's just as absurd to ignore our own hearts when we are experiencing brokenness and pain, trying to ignore it or hide it from others, attempting to continue to run this race of life as if nothing is wrong. It would be just as awkward and impossible as that man trying to run that marathon with a casted leg and crutches.

Identify the broken and hurting places in your life, love yourself well by sitting right down in the middle of them and cry out to God as you take your own paint brush (your faith in His ability to heal you), and apply His Blood to yourself. Watch as your own "holes" of hurt are sucked up by His Blood and fully filled with His resurrected life of completeness that is entirely yours.

> *For He is the complete fullness of Deity living in human form and our own completeness is now found in Him. We are completely filled with God as Christ's fullness overflows within us.* - Colossians 2:9-10 (TPT)

Gift yourself with the very necessary process of being completely filled, healed and made whole again. When the time is right, get up, and with unhindered hands, toss aside the cast and crutches, and run!

4
Jesus Had Stinky Feet

For a season of time, I was working the night shift in the ER unit in a couple of our local hospitals as an on-call, mobile psych assessor. My job was to assess patients who were admitted for various mental issues, whether they had tried to commit suicide, overdosed on drugs, alcohol poisoning, etc. I worked alongside the doctors to determine the best course of action for these patients, seeing people of all ages and all types of situations. I loved it. It was evangelism in the trenches at its finest.

One night, after I had worked from 11 p.m. to 4 a.m., just as I thought I could leave for the night, I was called on the floor to evaluate another patient. As I walked into the room, the stench was so horrible, I thought I might lose my dinner. Not only did this man wreak of alcohol, the odor from lack of hygiene, particularly coming from his feet, was almost unbearable.

This middle-aged man had made a mess of his life. He poisoned himself with alcohol, tried to commit suicide and plotted to take his brothers and own mother with him in the process. He was filled with so much hate, bitterness, and unforgiveness, yet at the same time, possessed a strange quietness.

His name was David. He had cuts all over his face and arms

from being heavily intoxicated and repeatedly falling. As I sat down by David's bed, knowing that my long night had just gotten longer, I suddenly was very aware of the Presence of Wonderful Jesus. I began to feel God's overwhelming love for David and Heaven's approval of him, yet at the same time, oddly enough, the stench of those feet!

As I pondered all this, I looked at his stinky, hole-filled socks and heard Jesus say, "Those are *My* feet, you know."

I was overcome with compassion for David. I wanted to see him the way Jesus did, and I knew I was receiving an invitation to peer through Heaven's lens. In loving this man, I knew I would be loving Jesus. Having this realization, I would have laid on David's feet if Jesus wanted me to. Those feet became so beautiful, so holy to me.

As David laid there, disheveled and restless, I began to tell him about David in the Bible. I told him story after story about the rascal he had been with Bathsheba, his plot to murder her husband and even the way his family had turned on him, too. I also told him he was the same man, who, as a young shepherd boy, believed His big God could kill a big giant. He was a worshipper who would quickly admit his mistakes, and the mightiest King that Israel had ever known. All of that was in the same man and all of Heaven never changed Its mind about him.

David laid his head back on the pillow as tears began to fall down his face. I asked if I could pray with him and prayed as if he was King David, declaring his true identity, peeling back the conversation Heaven wanted to have with him.

I don't know what happened to David after that night but

what I do know is this: Jesus was in the hospital that wintry night, with stinky Feet and hole-filled socks. . . and I never knew a smell could be so sweet.

> *Then the King will turn to the sheep on His right and say, 'You have a special place in my Father's heart. Come and experience the full inheritance of the kingdom realm that has been destined for you from before the foundation of the world! For when you saw Me hungry, you fed Me. When you found Me thirsty, you gave Me something to drink. When I had no place to stay, you invited Me in, and when I was poorly clothed, you covered Me. When I was sick, you tenderly cared for Me, and when I was in prison you visited Me.' "Then the Godly will answer Him, 'Lord, when did we see You hungry or thirsty and give You food and something to drink? When did we see You with no place to stay and invite You in? When did we see You poorly clothed and cover You? When did we see You sick and tenderly care for You, or in prison and visit You?' "And the King will answer them, 'Don't you know? When you cared for one of the least important of these My little ones, My true brothers and sisters, you demonstrated love for Me.*
>
> *- Matthew 25:34-40 (TPT)*

A few months ago, I drove about ten hours to see my eldest brother who was sick with cancer. They were not giving him much hope. God had performed a miracle for me (which I will share with you a little bit later) and I knew I wanted to share this miracle with him.

Now, plainly speaking, my brother had been quite the rascal most of his life. He made many decisions that hurt a lot of people and while extremely gifted, funny, and talented, he struggled with having the character and integrity to steward those giftings well. My brother's behavior was what would be described by many as that of a prodigal son. He didn't have relationship with some of his children and sadly, most had already made their judgments towards him, feeling as if "he got what he deserved." However, Heaven had something entirely different to say.

Due to his lifestyle of obscurity, I hadn't laid eyes on my brother in over twenty years. As I walked in his hospital room, this 6'4" man, who I knew growing up to be described by all the girls as "drop-dead gorgeous," was laying there, prematurely aged, frail and thin. His brown eyes grew wide as he looked up and I instantly came to his bedside for a long embrace. I forgave my precious brother a long time ago, wanting to see him healed and his life beautifully restored. We talked for quite some time and as we prayed, he surrendered his life to God, saying he forgave those he had been holding resentment against. It was beautiful.

A little while later, the nurse came in to administer his meds. As the pain killers began to kick in, he dozed off. I went in for the kill. As I laid my hand on his forehead, fully expecting him to get up, something I didn't expect happened. I sensed all of Heaven applauding, cheering, even wildly approving of this man. What? No fault-finding? No negativity, accusation or disapproval? Not a trace. I suddenly had the keen awareness I was laying my hands-on royalty. Completely undone by this, I continued to declare his healing, so much wanting my brother healed.

As I pondered what I experienced the next day, I heard the Lord say to me, "You know, Abigail, the voice in hell will always be that of accusation but the voice in Heaven is always that of acclamation."

Now, I don't use the word "acclamation" often, so when the Lord talks to me with fancy words, He's usually wanting me to take a deeper look. As I explored the word acclamation, I was stunned. The Google dictionary defines acclamation as "loud and enthusiastic approval, typically to welcome or honor someone or something."

Isn't that incredible? You see, the book of Revelation tells us that the enemy is the *"accuser of the brethren."* He's always throwing accusations toward us (the brethren), trying to get us to forget our identity as sons and daughters of the King. If he can get us to believe the ugly lie that our behavior is linked to our identity, then the weakening begins, and we start to lose our footing.

However, the voice in Heaven is always that of acclamation— loud and enthusiastic approval, cheering us on, encouraging us in our identity because who and Whose we are will never change, so Heaven never changes Its conversation on the matter either.

Friends, Jesus is too busy making intercession for you to be accusing you. That's enough to keep our praise and gratitude on for always.

> *So all of this magnifies the truth that we have a superior covenant with God than what they experienced, for Jesus Himself is its guarantor! Jesus permanently holds His Priestly office, since He lives forever and will never have a successor! He is able to save fully from now throughout eternity, everyone who comes to God through Him, because He lives to pray continually for*

*them. He is the High Priest Who perfectly fits our need
. . .* - Hebrews 7:22-26 (TPT)

If all of Heaven & Jesus aren't changing Their conversation
about you, let me ask you something, "Why are you?" What
does the conversation sound like between your ears? Pastor
Bill Johnson says something I love, "I can't afford to have a
thought about me that God doesn't have about me."

Jesus tells us how to pray in Matthew 6:10, *"Let Your
Kingdom come, let Your will be done on earth as it is in
Heaven"* (TPT). Instead of thinking about this as Heaven
being far away and earth being planet Earth, think about it
much more intimately. Paul tells us in Romans that the
Kingdom of God is righteousness, peace, and joy in the Holy
Spirit. Let His Kingdom be done on earth—your earth: your
mind, will, and emotions—as it already is in Heaven (your
born-again spirit), who you've always been and always will
be, the eternal you.

One time, the Lord said to me, "If you are not fully walking
in all I've created you to be, you are only partially loving
Me." May we love Him with our whole lives by believing Who
He fully is in us, for us, and through us and live entirely in
that reality.

Paul says in 2 Corinthians 4:7, *"We have this treasure in
earthen vessels. . ."* (ESV). In other words, Heaven wants to
find Its home in you. We don't put our furniture and our
most valuable possessions in the yard, outside, or on the
roof, do we? That would be quite odd. Well, how odd is it
to receive and believe His love for us only when we feel we
are "performing well," or doing everything right? That's like
partially moving in when the whole Kingdom is ours. Our

most valuable possessions are within our homes and our deepest treasures are tucked away, not easily and foolishly accessed.

Christ's eternal love for us, our identity as sons and daughters, the fullness of Him, living inside us, is the treasure within our earthen vessels. Colossians 2:9-10 says, *"For we are the complete fullness of Deity living in human form. And our own completeness is now found in Him. We are completely filled with God as Christ's fullness overflows within us"* (TPT).

In your mind, are you sitting in the recliner of this truth? By "sitting," I mean, have you entirely found a resting place for your heart here? Isaiah 30:15 says, *"In returning and rest you shall be saved; in quietness and in trust shall be your strength. . ."* (ESV). Our whole lives are to be lived from this place of forever truth.

Oh friend, all of Heaven's sound over you is pure acclamation because of your identity as a son or daughter, not in your behavior. My actions didn't give me my family's last name, my birthright did.

The more you fully embrace your royal identity, any beggarly behavior still lingering will take care of itself. Believe it, receive it, straighten your crown, and fully walk in the birthright that is yours through the Name that is above all names, the First and the Last, the Beginning and the End. By the way, has anyone ever told you that you look just like your Daddy?

The Conversation In Heaven

5
An Invitation Into The Fellowship of His Sufferings

Earlier, I shared with you the benefits of having a Sozo. Even with all the hard work involved in obtaining my master's degree in counseling, one of the most effective tools I've seen help people the most did not happen in a classroom but through all I learned from Sozo training.

Oftentimes, when we have been deeply wounded by something or someone in our life we compartmentalize that pain. In a way, this stunts our emotional and mental growth because of the pain we haven't allowed ourselves to face, or pain we simply feel we can't face.

A Sozo session can be very effective because through guided, trained counsel, and intentional questions, you are invited to allow God in to help you face that pain and through His amazing love, encounter Him. Many, many times, healing is experienced so deeply, where years of traditional counseling and medication may have failed.

One thing that occurs in a Sozo session is when the issue that needs to be dealt with is made clear, the Sozo counselor will ask you, "Where do you see Jesus?" You are then to look in your heart and see if you can literally identify Jesus in the scene. While this may sound strange, believe me, it is totally and brilliantly legit. Where there has been extreme trauma, this may take a while. Many times, there is a wall of unforgiveness, resentment, etc., that can temporarily block you from seeing Him.

I love Sozo experiences so much because one or sometimes two more people are there, whose sole purpose is to pray for you until you are brought to a place of breakthrough and freedom where you can clearly see Jesus for yourself. I personally believe it's one of the most powerful tools of inner healing available.

One time, I personally experienced an amazing encounter and absolute breakthrough in a Sozo session. My divorce, as I mentioned earlier, was very, very painful. I share this story not for assumptions to be made about the situation but in an effort for you to understand this as one of the most painful, traumatic events in my entire life.

River, my son, was about eight at the time and my daughter, Lily Grace, was seven. I remember standing in my mother's driveway, about to go pick up my children after a weekend visit with their father. We had prearranged to meet at 6:00 p.m. I was looking forward to getting them home and ready for school the next day, tucking them into bed as usual. Just then, I received a text informing me that he would not be meeting me with our children and to check my email. As I opened the email, to my horror, I read the unimaginable.

I was informed I would not be seeing my children that night. I was also told I must fight a legal battle involving my children, a battle that ended up costing more than $20,000. I was told I would need to obtain witnesses as I read hurtful and outlandish lies through tear-filled eyes of disbelief.

In a moment, my world came crashing down. For the next five days I did not know where my children were, was unable to speak to them, and did not know when I would get to see them again. As I finished reading this email full of lies and betrayal, I fell to my knees in the driveway and from the deepest part of my being, let out a gut-wrenching cry I didn't know was humanly possible. I kneeled there in my pajamas, for what seemed like hours, a sobbing heap of pain, consumed with the agony of betrayal, loss, and fear, totally unable to navigate.

Now, you must understand. I had a home birth with one of my children and blended up their baby food from organic fruits and veggies. I homeschool them, and since they were born, have arranged my life to ensure I'm able to be home to raise them. I have completely loved and enjoyed a great sense of fulfillment being their mom, even on the not-so-fun days.

Truth was revealed in a few weeks from that time, but the fight and process was excruciating and terrifying. I remember feeling like a failure because I thought divorce would ruin my kids, like I had completely failed as their mom by not just sticking it out.

I have watched as my children have experienced the beautiful, healing power of Jesus in their own tender hearts in ways that keep me continually amazed. At twelve and fourteen, they are the most tender, powerful, and precious kids. I enjoy every minute of our beautiful lives together.

Oh friends, never underestimate the ability of the nurturing Holy Spirit to keep your children in their own journey. We cannot shield them from some kinds of pain they will endure but we can completely trust our God to use it to fortify their hearts as they are being beautifully and brilliantly built into strong castles, able to endure all seasons of life's weather with all the awe and wonder that comes from simply being a castle. On top of that, your children will encounter others who will find refuge inside the walls of their story from their own storms. We mustn't abort this process or doubt the Holy Spirit's ability within our children to process pain. It would be like trying to clip the cocoon of their hearts, thus stunting their own emergence and ability to fly with wings that reveal a butterfly, a transformation that is as wondrous as it is glorious.

Back to the driveway in my pajamas. As I kneeled there, sobbing, I remember wondering why my mom didn't come out and console me, and to compound the pain, where was my Jesus in this God-forsaken moment? I just sat there, weeping and in shock; feeling alone, abandoned, and helpless.

I tucked the trauma of this entire experience deep, deep in my heart. My dear sister's death would happen in just a few months and simultaneously I would be hurled into a fierce divorce battle with no feasible way to process the kind of pain I was experiencing.

Fast forward to my Sozo session. As we began to pray, I sensed that this event was what God wanted to discuss. I remember all the trauma, pain, and loss emerging to the top of my heart with a vengeance. I realized that I had been harboring anger not only towards my mom but also towards God. Why would He have allowed such insurmountable pain and why did she not come out and comfort me in the driveway?

While I was in that session, dealing with all the anger and hurt, the Sozo counselor asked me where Jesus was. I couldn't see Jesus at all. As I kept my eyes closed, all I could see and feel was pain; an angry, red, hazy fog of pain. As they kept praying, the red fog began to slowly clear. They kept praying and I kept trying to see Him in that scene in my mom's driveway.

Suddenly, I felt the room where we were, getting brighter and brighter. I kept my eyes tightly closed because I knew something was happening and I didn't want to move a muscle. I literally began to feel the tangible Presence of Jesus in the room. I heard the women around me get quieter as we all sensed Him. At the same time, inside myself, that angry, red fog kept clearing until I saw Him. He was standing in the doorway of my mom's home. He was looking at me as I wept in the driveway, His arm outstretched.

Suddenly, I had an encounter with Him right there in that room. He said, "Abigail, the reason I wouldn't allow your Mom to come to you was because *I* was there. You have enjoyed and experienced the power of My resurrection, yet, in that moment I was inviting you into the fellowship of My sufferings."

I immediately fell on my face and wept deeper than I had in a long, long time. I just kept saying, "I didn't know, Jesus, I didn't know that You were there, inviting me into a deeper place with You. I didn't know. . . I didn't know."

Even now I find it hard to put into words, but I sensed such a love, honor, and awe to be invited into that place with Him. My entire perspective of what seemed to be the greatest experience of pain in my life was suddenly turned into the most beautiful door of greater intimacy, of deeper friendship with my Jesus. It was as if He was inviting me to know parts of Him along the road of suffering ahead, for reasons I may never understand, that couldn't have been known or realized any other way, a depth of relationship with Him that had no shortcut.

My victimized pain was changed into the greatest sense of honor. Honor to be invited by Him into my own Garden of Gethsemane, where He was beckoning me, even wooing me, side by side with Him! Gethsemane comes from a Greek word meaning "oil press." Christ Himself did not avoid the pressing, becoming the Eternal Oil of salvation for all mankind. If the garden of Gethsemane in my own life is where He can be found, there is no other garden I'd rather be in. I cried out in repentance and expressed my love and gratitude to Him for the realization of this invitation.

When the whole experience was over, and I finally opened my eyes, the other women in the room were a mess. They later told me they saw the whole room become brighter and that they couldn't touch me. They said they just watched as I had this holy encounter with wonderful, wonderful Jesus. Later, the Sozo leader said she had never experienced anything like that before in all her years of this type of inner healing.

How enriched are they who find their strength in the Lord; within their hearts are the highways of holiness! Even when their paths wind through the dark valley of tears, they dig deep to find a pleasant pool where others find only pain.
He gives to them a brook of blessing, filled from the rain of an outpouring. They grow stronger and stronger with every step forward.

- Psalm 84:5-6 (TPT)

What looks to be debilitating and crippling in your life may be an invitation to find Him precisely there; to encounter Him in such a way that your own "dark valley of tears," becomes a doorway of growth and healing, a door that will open again to the bright land of hope. As you allow yourself this process of being dug deeper in Him, you will emerge again, even though you feel as if you might die there. Rest assured that when you come up out of that place, you will discover that your own "pleasant pool," has now sprung up within. A pool in which you will be able to give "others who only find pain," a fresh drink. A drink from the deep pool that you have allowed to be dug inside of you, deep within the soil of your broken heart.

When your will is surrendered as a "laid down lover" upon Heaven's altar, your life's experiential, painful dirt, transforms into a pool that has been dug so deep in your soul that a "brook of blessing" is now able to emerge; a brook where others will be able to drink deeply and be refreshed with renewed hope, coming from the desert or the greenest of meadows. Hope that flows eternal and free from Heaven's altar, joyfully winding its way through your surrendered heart—becoming an extravagant deluge on all who encounter you.

41

Jesus told the very thirsty and pain-filled woman at the well, "whoever drinks of the water that I will give him will never be thirsty again.

The water that I will give him will become in him a spring of water welling up to eternal life. He shall be forever satisfied.

- John 4:14 (ESV/TPT)

From the beginning of time, Jesus has meant for the well of Himself to be refreshingly alive inside of us; no blockage and no contamination. A well springing up for others to enjoy, to find refreshment and to be healed. Let the transformation begin in you first, so others can drink from Him Who springs up within, fully alive and well, inside of you.

Dear friend, as you read this, if a memory of trauma or pain is being highlighted to you, I invite you now to ask Jesus where He was in your pain. Simply wait for His answer. If you feel you aren't getting any response, ask your heart if there is a wall there.

Without realizing it, we build walls around our hearts as self-protection mechanisms, which is the whole point of a wall. A wall is built up around the memory of a traumatic event, deep unforgiveness, hate, shame, etc. During that kind of trauma or pain, we are incapable of dealing adequately with what's going on. As a coping strategy, we put up these walls to protect ourselves from the deep pain we are experiencing, like the way a person deals with pain from a car wreck or significant bodily injury. That person won't initially feel the pain due to the surge of adrenaline shooting through their body, protecting them from the existing pain they cannot bear.

When we feel our lives are threatened, we develop an instinctive defense against danger. The term "fight or flight," is often associated with circumstances where this type of adrenaline is released into the body. If our physical bodies respond in this protective manner, is it too hard to believe the emotional and mental parts of us do as well? Even in extreme cases of multiple personalities, etc., this is just another way our soul is attempting to deal with various forms of pain.

Oh friend, will you trust God to be enough for that problem or pain? Are you doubting that He is enough for you, that He is safe enough for you to let that wall of self-protection down?

It's okay if you're not there yet. Trust takes time and relationship. If you allow God in, He will get you there. If there is something separating you from experiencing healing and freedom, there has probably been a wall built there, whether you are able to identify it or not. It's okay if you don't know what that wall may be. I promise, His great love for you will show you. Just open your heart and fully allow Him in. You can entirely trust that He will not invite you into something He does not intend to see all the way through with you to your complete healing.

Oh friend, you can camp out on His faithfulness. He is forever the safest Person you will ever know, ever trust and ever love. He is the only One who knows you best yet loves you most. Your tender heart can find its resting place and forever home in Him.

I am standing in absolute stillness, silent before the One I love, waiting as long as it takes for Him to rescue me. Only God is my Savior, and He will not fail me. For He alone is my safe Place. His wrap-around Presence always protects me as my Champion Defender. There's no risk of failure with God! So why would I let worry paralyze me, even when troubles multiply around me?

God's glory is all around me! His wrap-around Presence is all I need, for the Lord is my Savior, my Hero, and my life-giving Strength. Join me, everyone! Trust only in God every moment!
Tell Him all your troubles and pour out your heart-longings to Him. Believe me when I tell you—He will help you! - Psalm 62:5-8 (TPT)

6
Keep Hope Alive by Scrubbing a Bathtub

A few years ago, in my valley of brokenness, hurt, and loss, the kids and I moved to what is now our home and much-loved community. We have rebuilt our lives here and I am so grateful for the people who have literally become our family and a church we know will forever be ours.

When we first moved here, I did not know all the goodness that would be found in this great land. All I felt was devastation and trembling vulnerability as I obediently put one foot in front of the other to the Father's voice in coming here. I was so raw in my emotions and being among all these people I didn't know, caused me to feel exposed; yet my desire for healing and wholeness outweighed my fear or insecurity of what anyone would think. Being a pastor myself for over fifteen years, I didn't much care what church folk thought of me. Oh friend, when your desire to get out of the boat and see Jesus outweighs the scary height of the waves, walking on water becomes possible.

I was so grateful we found our home church, enrolled myself in ministry school while continuing in my master's program, and newly committed to homeschooling my children, all at the same time. Believe me, it was a humbling experience to submit myself to teachers younger than me in this ministry school, but I knew God was in it, so did it really matter? I think I would have submitted myself to a toddler if it meant further healing and wholeness.

At times, we get too caught up in all the clean lines we think need to be drawn in our lives, the neat boxes we unconsciously stack up. God never meant for us to live closed-off, with hurt and pain causing us to keep ourselves neatly packed away, hidden, and restrained on so many levels. God is all about busting out of those boxes and freeing us to live wide-open, seen and known, honest, healed and whole lives. It's the only way we can truly enjoy this gift called life and for others to be able to enjoy the gift we are as well. In all that unresolved hurt and pain, the last thing we can think we are to anybody, is a gift.

This type of thinking must be transformed through the healing process Jesus will lead us into; sometimes, through a desert-like season.

I remember for a long time feeling like when I looked out on my life, all I could see was ugly, red dirt, with a huge, unfair, yellow bulldozer sitting right in the middle of the torn-up field of my life. No trace of green grass, just ugly dirt that seemed to have devoured any trace of the life-filled, green grass that used to be there, with that bulldozer so assumingly, presumptuously and unfairly parked right in the center.

There's no way to shortcut the process of new growth and life being able to be realized in our lives. Just like a tree must be pruned back to bear even greater fruit, there will be times in our lives when deep hurt and loss are experienced. It can feel and seem as if all is being torn up, no evidence of life or new growth anywhere— just the pain of what would have been, what could have been, and what we feel should have been.

However, in the faithfulness that is eternally characteristic of our Father-Creator, the One who knows us best and loves us most, we will eventually begin to see through the pain and discover the Silhouette of a Beautiful Man, climbing up into the driver's seat of that bulldozer. We will discover the bulldozer to no longer be a sign of pain but of loving purpose. Purpose that has new life within its wheels, signifying Heaven's eternal and loving intention to do what is needed for growth and life for our future.

A bulldozer doesn't show up in any field without removing what is no longer useful and making way for a beautiful, new foundation; a planting and trustworthy harvest that is eternal.

Our Father comes as the great, wise, loving and tender Gardener. We can place all our trembling trust in Him, with full assurance that no matter how sharp the blade He carries, His love-filled intention only prunes what will hinder growth, what will hinder fruitfulness and fullness in our lives. In John 15, Jesus speaks of this very thing:

> *I am a true sprouting Vine, and the Farmer who tends the vine is my Father. He cares for the branches connected to Me by lifting and propping up the fruitless branches and pruning every fruitful branch to yield a greater harvest. The words I have spoken over you have already cleansed you. So, you must remain in life-union with Me, for I remain in life-union with you. For as a*

branch severed from the vine will not bear fruit, so your life will be fruitless unless you live your life intimately joined to Mine...As you live in union with Me as your source, fruitfulness will stream from within you—but when you live separated from Me you are powerless...if you live in life-union with Me and if My words live powerfully within you—then you can ask whatever you desire and it will be done. When your lives bear abundant fruit, you demonstrate that you are My mature disciples who glorify My Father! I love each of you with the same love that the Father loves Me. You must continually let My love nourish your hearts. If you keep My commands, you will live in My love, just as I have kept My Father's commands, for I continually live nourished and empowered by His love. My purpose for telling you these things is so that the joy that I experience will fill your hearts with overflowing gladness! - John 15:1-11 (TPT)

It was the lovely month of April. The month that brings Spring and with it comes all things green, all things that speak newness of life. We had just gotten a lovely, little, white baby goat, named Sophia. Oh how the kids and I loved her! She was the perfect picture of innocence and play. Her face was pure white with sweet and trusting eyes. We fed her from a bottle and would let her in the house while the kids did their homeschool work. She would curl up in the chair next to them and wait until their recess. She wore a little bell we could hear as she skipped outside in the yard.

One day, when I briefly left the house, the neighbor let his dogs out of their fence. Minutes later, when I returned, to my horror, I found her laying in the yard, wounded and not breathing. I remember kneeling there, sobbing over this precious animal. I realized she had symbolized so much hope in my heart. Hope for innocence and carefree happiness to return. Hope for new life and joy to spring up. Suddenly and so unfairly, she was gone, unjustly taken from our lives. Gone. Just like what seemed to be the perfect life I thought I had, the life that felt unjustly taken from me; yet another picture of that bulldozer, sitting in the middle of my field, glaring at me in mockery.

As I wept, I realized I had a commitment that day. I knew this friend would understand if I cancelled but something inside me felt compelled to keep it. In a few minutes, I showed up at her house. At the time, this friend was an acquaintance I admired from a distance. We were cultivating a friendship in its early stages. Truthfully, I felt a mixture of intimidation, admiration, and love for her. Our relationship had not yet grown to the point where a deep, eternal love would soon swallow up the other unhealthy emotions I was feeling, due to my hurt and fear. A deeper friendship would soon be cultivated, a sister relationship that I could only dream was in my near future with this woman, a friend I would love as my own soul, like Jonathan did David.

She and her husband are leaders at our church. For a season of time, I felt moved to clean her house. I would go every other week and scrub floors, toilets, bathtubs, etc. It felt awkward and I wasn't sure she would allow me to do this. I'm so glad she did because something deeper, something eternal was taking place.

I knew later why I felt compelled to keep the commitment I had made that very day, only minutes after losing baby

Sophia. I had a destined date, a conversation with Heaven to be had.

As I scrubbed her bathtub and wept over Sophia, I was overwhelmed with sadness as I looked around at her beautiful life. She has a wonderful husband, precious family and models healthy ministry. She is esteemed by so many as she does what she loves. I was overcome with sadness. I had all this once. A nice, beautiful, house we had remodeled, a vibrant church we were pastoring, the love and respect of our community, the pitter patter of little feet growing in our home, family portraits all over the walls. It was like I was staring in the rear-view mirror of what used to be my life. Now look at me, scrubbing a bathtub of my "used to be's." Why is this my life? What have I done to deserve all this?

Amidst feeling so much pain, it was difficult to see a trace of God at all. Why am I here, God? Do these people even care to know me? Do they even know who I used to be? The love and respect we used to have? The good thing we had going? Where did my calling go? Who would ever want to hear me preach the gospel again? No one around here even knows who I used to be. A woman of strength and influence, a woman people loved and respected. Now, all I feel people know or see me to be is a hurting, broken, struggling, single mom.

As I sat there, bent over that tub, a broken mess, I continued scrubbing and weeping. It's as if I felt all of hell mocking me. Why would a loving Heavenly Father ask me to do something that seemed so cruel, as if to dangle in front of me all I used to love and enjoy, only to realize it's no longer mine?

All at once, I was infused with a stubbornness of intention to scrub harder, scrub as if the enamel of the tub would come right off! As I scrubbed, I heard the conversation of Heaven draw near, the breath of the Father forming words of liberation in my heart. I felt His invitation to find Him right here, on this bathroom floor; to listen to His Voice here, as I'm bent over this tub, an invitation for me to mourn yet another necessary layer of loss while at the same time, beckoning me to turn the knob of Heaven to another, door of hope. A hope urging me to keep scrubbing, keep sowing into family, into ministry, into all that seemed to taunt me of what *was* because this is, *my yet to be*.

I began to be filled with such love and thankfulness as I felt all of Heaven wildly encouraging me to keep scrubbing. Cheering me on to scrub to keep hope breathing. I felt the nearness of Jesus saying, "You do this because it keeps hope alive. It keeps hope alive of what I have called you to do, Abigail. My Voice has never changed the subject in your life." I had a keen awareness that by doing this, I was sowing into eternal currency of the Kingdom, not dictated by anything of this natural and earthly realm.

In 1 Kings 17, a widow with a young son lived in a town called Zarephath. The prophet Elijah is told to go there, that the Lord has instructed a widow to feed him. When he arrives, he finds the widow gathering sticks and asks her for bread and water. She tells him that due to the famine she has no baked bread, only a handful of flour in a jar and a little bit of oil. In her great sorrow, she says she's going to make it for herself, her son and then prepare to die. Elijah tells her not to be afraid, to go and do what she has planned but to make him a small cake first.

How insolent, we might think! Where's the compassion and comfort? However, Elijah knew that she had an opportunity to make an exchange with Heaven's currency. He was setting her up for a miracle, inviting her to hear the conversation in Heaven to keep hope alive. In doing so, she experienced breakthrough; not just her own but for her whole family as well.

Elijah tells her the flour and the jar of oil would not run out, and it didn't—for years. With no hope, scarcity, and death all around, she reached through the portal of Heaven, tapped into eternal Hope, and through her obedience, saved her entire household.

Oh friend, have you ever felt like that widow? You know, the voice of self-pity is never heard in Heaven. It doesn't exist. As hurtful and difficult as your situation may be right now, Heaven is always singing the song of hope, setting you up for a miracle, for your own breakthrough and the breakthrough of those around you.

What I was doing that day in scrubbing that beautiful bathtub, I was doing to break free; to be reminded of the hope of my calling, and to keep that hope stirred up and alive in my heart and mind. I suddenly was able to look at my dear friend, Jenn's life, through Heaven's lens. I *get* to sow into Jenn. She's one of the greatest, most anointed preachers I have ever known. Her most beautiful pulpit is the authentic life she lives entirely for Jesus. What she carries began to stoke and keep the hunger and hope alive for the calling in my own life that had never stopped speaking, the treasure I never stopped carrying—whether I could feel it, see it, or believe it.

Heaven was preaching back to me, "You're doing this to stay free, Abigail. Keep sowing into what I've called you to do because it doesn't have anything to do with you, or your circumstances, or the things you can't change. It has everything to do with My eternal Word over your life."

I couldn't help but feel overwhelmed with a newfound freedom. I was filled with such fresh hope from Heaven, knowing I was involved in an eternal transaction, with a currency not of this world. Sitting there on that bathroom floor of hurt, I began to pour out thanks to God as right before my eyes, ashes had been traded for Heaven's beauty.

I started to realize that what My Father had asked me to do wasn't cruel at all. He lovingly wanted me to break new ground, inviting me into the process through obedience. I discovered that bathroom floor to be the beautiful soil of Heaven, the breeding ground for new growth in my life. Fresh, green grass was peeking up from the red, broken up, earthy dirt of my own life. The bulldozer I thought to be cruel, was turning up its hope-filled engine with loving intention and eternal purpose. It was the season of Spring after all, in Heaven and in my own earth.

The Conversation In Heaven

7
Heaven's Waiting Room

I have always been involved in health and fitness. Losing my father to cancer at the tender age of sixteen, caused me to begin to be proactive in my own health. My Dad was such a great man. There are five girls and one boy in my family. We were an unstoppable, one-family basketball and softball team, with my dad as the coach. He was a very passionate man but struggled to manage stress well. He developed cancer at age forty-one and fought a very brave battle for the next eight years. Sadly, cancer had run in both sides of our family, losing other loved ones to its despicable grasp. We recently buried my brother who also lost his battle to this wretched disease.

As kids, we weren't told many details about my dad's fight. He was in and out of surgeries so frequently, we didn't think much of it. He'd bounce back and keep going. However, behind the scenes, it was getting increasingly worse. My dad was a young, heart-wrenching, forty-eight years old when he died. There was a packed house at his funeral. He was a well-respected leader in our community and church, loved by so many. I can't imagine what family and friends must have felt that October day as they saw six kids walk down the center aisle of the church where we grew up and take our seats on the front row, my mom sitting there, now left a young widow.

I believed for my dad's healing until he drew his last breath. I loved him so very much. He squeezed every drop of passion out of life. He rewrote his own history as a beautiful example of a hands-on dad, despite not having the same experience with his own father.

Being the middle child, my dad would stick up for me when needed and certainly knew how to have fun. There was a lot of activity always going on in our home. Kids were always over, somebody was constantly playing a sport, siblings going in five different directions. I don't remember much quiet time. My dad's presence no longer there left a gaping, aching hole. However, I experienced God to be faithful to His promise in Psalm 68:5-6:

A Father of the fatherless and a Defender of the widows is God in His holy habitation (JUB).

My relationship with my mom flourished after my dad's passing. We weren't very close prior to his death but as a sixteen-year-old, after dad died, I began to sleep most nights with her. My mom has a beautiful relationship with God. She has always lived with a child-like faith that has left an eternal imprint on my own relationship with Him. I remember one morning she told me she felt tangible arms holding her in the night. I witnessed the Husband side of God be so real to my mom during this time and His nature as *Abba* (Daddy) came to my rescue time after time.

After a necessary time of grieving, my mom began to host a Bible study for widows and widowers in our home. By nature, my mom is shy, and I knew this was a big step for her. However, Heaven was pleased with her sacrifice. A few months later, a wonderful, gentle, loving man, who had buried his wife months prior, came into her life through this Bible study. Howard soon took on the role of a kind and gentle step-father to all of us as teenagers, for many years to come. He was exactly what we needed.

I have found it interesting that often in our life, when we choose to sow into others' pain, as my Mom did, even when we are experiencing pain ourselves, it's like all the attention of Heaven is captivated by such a selfless sacrifice and the dump trucks of blessing begin to fill our own backyard. This truth is echoed in Psalm 126:5-6:

> *Restore our fortunes, Lord, as streams renew the desert. Those who sow in tears shall reap in joy. He who continually goes forth weeping, bearing seed for sowing, shall doubtless come again with rejoicing, bringing his sheaves with him.* (NKJV)

One time, the Holy Spirit showed me a picture about this. He showed me a farmer sowing seed, happily skipping down each row as he dropped his seed in the ground. The next farmer sowed his seed, walking down each row, but his shoulders were slumped and sadness was in his heart, yet he continued to put his seed in the ground. The third farmer was even sadder, tears streaming down his face as he walked down each row, yet, still, he sowed his seed.

The Lord asked me if all the seed went into the ground, despite the countenance, emotion or mood of each farmer. I answered that it certainly went into the ground. He then told me Heaven had every seed accounted for. Oh friend, as we keep sowing, happy or sad, joy or pain, we can rest assured, knowing Heaven is taking inventory and will care for our hearts and heal our emotions in the process, setting us up for a beautiful harvest, one we will experience and enjoy in our own lives, just like the obedient farmer bringing his sheaves (rewarding fruit) with him.

However, self-pity has no room for giving; it's what it is: self-PITy. It keeps you trapped, self-centered, isolated and closed off. No river can flow there, and no life can be fully lived there. You see, friends, Heaven's resources are limitless, lidless, bottomless. On our best day, we cannot exhaust them. Why not live a life poured out, a life with both hands outstretched in wild surrender? This kind of life unlocks the currency of Heaven to always make transactions through us and for us. This is one of my favorite joys of Kingdom living. It's a great adventure to be experienced and a powerful truth to give away.

In April 2016, my mom was diagnosed with breast cancer. I remember staying the night with her in the hospital after surgery, praying wild prayers that a new breast would grow in the place of the one removed. I had so much faith for that to happen. Even though it didn't, she healed just fine and is doing well. Oddly enough, I remember feeling pain in my own left breast that night in the hospital.

Having a strong background in psychology, I dismissed it as "sympathy" pain. The pain worsened. Two months later, I was teaching one of my usual, community-wide boot camps and began to feel sluggish and just a bit off. I started to favor that side of my body when I would sleep at night and soon, I was waking up, grabbing ice to relieve the pain. Obviously, I knew then, something wasn't right, so I went in for a check-up. I remember walking into the room and feeling such a great peace carried by the nurse seeing me. She was this tender, kind, yet strong, faith-filled woman.

Right away she scheduled a mammogram which turned into an ultrasound which turned into an all-day camp out at the hospital.

It seemed surreal after walking through these exact steps with my mom, just two months prior. The doctor came in and while expressing his concern about the size of the mass in my left breast, saying it was one of the largest he had ever seen, he wasn't that concerned because he thought it could just be a very common, fibroid mass, given my age and healthy fitness level. He wanted to schedule a biopsy to be sure.

Two days later, I was walking into a biopsy. I had such a peace that morning. I remember being more concerned about missing my boot campers' class than I was being in a hospital gown, surrounded by pink ribbons and breast torture machines.

As they began the biopsy, it was just me in the room with the doctor and nurse. Out of my left eye, I could see a crazy-long needle coming toward me, yet I found myself humming, "Great is Thy Faithfulness." I knew Heaven was singing this over me, so I joined in. I hummed that hymn the entire procedure. What is historically known for most women as very painful, I remember as an experience governed by peace.

That was a warm Friday in June. When I returned home from the procedure, I sat on my front porch swing, pondering. I knew I was about to walk through something difficult, yet I didn't really feel fear, just a strong knowing that it seemed as if a trespasser was clinging to my body. That's the only way I can explain it—a trespasser.

That entire weekend was literally a waiting game.

I've learned something about waiting from Heaven's perspective. Waiting doesn't have to be torture, friends. Heaven's waiting room is never filled with feet that are anxiously and fearfully pacing back and forth, so neither should the waiting room of our hearts. David talks about waiting through the lens of Heaven in Psalm 71:1-3:

> *I waited and waited and waited some more, patiently, knowing God would come through for me. Then, at last, He bent down and listened to my cry. He stooped down to lift me out of danger, from the desolate pit I was in, out of the muddy mess I had fallen into. Now He's lifted me up into a firm, secure place and steadied me while I walk along His ascending path. A new song for a new day rises in me every time I think about how He breaks through for me! Ecstatic praise pours out of my mouth until everyone hears how God has set me free. Many will see His miracles; they'll stand in awe of God and fall in love with Him!* (TPT)

As I waited for the biopsy results that long weekend, I knew there was a battle I would be fighting; one I must fully trust my King to carry me through. My safest battle stance would not be in picking up a striving sword but rather a flag of surrendered trust. A surrendering to the One Who is worthy of my entire trust, my entire life and my entire future. This place of surrender was the safest place I had ever known, the place where Peace reigned supreme, the place where all my questions were laid to rest. As I waited for results that weekend, in my heart, over and over, I just kept hearing the song by Kristen DiMarco, "Take Courage."

Take courage my heart, stay steadfast my soul
He's in the waiting, He's in the waiting.
Hold onto your hope as your triumph unfolds
He's never failing, He's never failing . . .

I knew this was the song being sung over me in the waiting room of Heaven so while I waited, why not keep myself and all my emotions in that room as well? If Heaven wasn't worried, wasn't pacing back and forth, why should I?

We must remember, friends, Heaven is not confined to the time and space of this earthly realm so "worry because I'm in a hurry" or "I need an answer, an explanation now," doesn't exist there. 1 Corinthians 13 describes the very first attribute of love to be patience. If your life always feels like stress, hurry, or urgent, back up and find where love is. Rebuild your life from that place. The place of peace is seldom hurry, and certainly, never scurry.

When we experience seasons of waiting in our lives, instead of expecting them to be difficult, why not choose to step into the same waiting room with all of Heaven? I can assure you in that room there is no anxiety, no difficulty, no fear, and no bad report. Oh friend, if we could just learn to partner with Heaven in every step of our life, on every changing terrain, in every season, we will always have what we need for every situation, no matter how scary, difficult, or insurmountable it feels.

Heaven always has something to say about you and your circumstance, something to give, but are we listening? By really listening, we position our hearts to receive everything we will ever need in and for any situation we may face.

You may be reading this thinking, it can't be this simple but I'm telling you, friend, it is. We make these kinds of things harder than they need to be. I know because I've done it many times and it is miserable any other way than His.

Did you know you can train yourself to hear what Heaven is saying? It's not as difficult as you might think. It could be as simple as a song you start to hear out of the blue, maybe one you haven't heard since you were a child, or a phrase you keep hearing, a friend's voice of encouragement, or even a random love song that keeps playing itself over and over in your heart. It could be more intentional on your part, like making yourself stay in a passage of Scripture until your emotions line up with the unchanging truth on the pages.

No matter the avenue, pay attention to these seeming subtle and insignificant things. They are anything but that. This is Heaven talking to you, encouraging you, and coaching you to come up higher, up above the clouds of your circumstances where the Son is always shining. It is the Voice of Heaven, inviting you to hear what is being said about your situation, inviting you to see what Heaven is seeing, and feel what Heaven is feeling, offering you to take it as your own. All the encouragement, faith, and strength you will need is found here. This is the game changer, my friends. This is us partnering with exactly what Jesus taught us to do in Matthew 6 when we pray.

When you pray, there is no need to repeat empty phrases, praying like those who don't know God, for they expect God to hear them because of their many words. There is no need to imitate them, since your

Father already knows what you need before you ask Him... Pray like this: Our Father in Heaven, hallowed be Your Name. Your kingdom come, Your will be done on earth as it is in heaven. - Matthew 6: 7-10 (TPT)

First thing that Monday morning, I received a phone call from the radiologist. "Well, Ms. Jennings, what do you think this is?"

I responded, "Why don't you tell me what I know it is?"

He replied, "It is what we feared. It's cancer."

I heard this news as I was on one of my walks in my driveway that winds through the big, open field to my house. This had become my favorite place to pray and commune with God, most of the time in my pajamas. I loved to look up at the blue, open sky and just pour my heart out to Him. Oh friends, we must develop a life that is prayer. Do you know what I mean?

Don't be pulled in different directions or worried about a thing. Be saturated in prayer throughout each day, offering your faith-filled requests before God with overflowing gratitude. Tell Him every detail of your life, then God's wonderful peace that transcends human understanding, will make the answers known to you through Jesus Christ. - Philippians 4:6-7 (TPT)

Let joy be your continual feast. Make your life a prayer. And in the midst of everything be always giving thanks, for this is God's perfect plan for you in Christ Jesus.
                              - 1 Thessalonians 5:16-18 (TPT)

Now, believe me, many years of my life were spent worrying about things first and "freak out" praying as one of my panic button options. This is not the way He wants us to live the abundant life purchased for us. The answer to anxiety and what we experience as anxiety attacks is not pills in a bottle but the medicine we give ourselves by opening our mouths and pouring our hearts out to Father God, the One Who is Peace. We mustn't ever let our vocabulary be damaged by our pain. *"Let the redeemed of the Lord, SAY so, whom He has redeemed from trouble"* Psalm 107:2 (ESV).

I cannot tell you the times I would walk my long driveway, speaking out loud, sometimes even shouting out the Psalms, many times through tears, intentionally reminding myself of the truth when my circumstances and emotions were trying to choke every ounce of air I had with fear and anxiety.

We can release the chokehold of those enemies by opening our mouths and speaking out the promises of God. This is one of the greatest, most underutilized weapons we have to experiencing and enjoying a life of victory and peace. The weapon and often, the miracle needed, is in your mouth. In Psalm 103:5, David speaks of our God Who helps us keep miracles in our mouths, *"Who satisfies your mouth with good things so that your youth is renewed like the eagles"* (NKJV).

Even our vitality and youth being renewed are linked to the words He has satisfied and already made good for us.

The empowering news is that this is a choice we get to make, not a feeling we follow. Do you know what I mean, dear friend? You always have the choice to speak out the truth, to stand and believe God's Word and what Heaven is saying, even when circumstances are trying to dictate the obvious facts. When you speak out into your atmosphere, the Word of God, the truth He is showing you, your body hears it and your emotions must line up with it. As you speak, those words are sent out to create that truth. If our Creator-God used words to build the world we enjoy, to create humanity, as His son or daughter, why would you not believe your words carry the designing capability and sound of your Father to do the same? I'm telling you, it works. Maybe not on your first try, or your second but keep saying it, believing it and keep doing it.

1 Thessalonians 5:17 says, *"make your life a continual prayer."* We were born to be in constant communication with our Father, to enjoy a deep, authentic, intimate relationship with Him. We are wired this way, so anything that would try to interrupt our Heavenly communication and relationship is like a bad signal. It's like experiencing fuzzy cell phone service and saying, "I'm sorry, I can't hear you, it's breaking up, we seem to have a bad connection."

When we go days without our face in His Word, spending alone time with Him, it's like trying to live our life with a garbled, bad signal. No one can make a decision or have any rich, meaningful communication with a bad connection. Heaven's signal is always crystal clear. What about on your end?

To love and know Him, is to love His Word. Clear up bad connections or fuzzy reception by keeping your face in the Word. Live like an intoxicated person on His Word, with full permission to be a binge drinker within the Pages.

So, here I am, being told I have breast cancer, as I walk my favorite path, with our big, fat pig, Wilb*her*, waddling beside me, several of our sweet chickens clucking around, and our plump, white cat, Pumpkin, lazily sunbathing. As a single Mom whose livelihood is made by various forms of physical fitness, if I don't show up for my clients, I don't get paid. I realized I would need surgery and recovery time. For the most part, I am self-employed, with no paid time off. Extravagant health insurance for me and my family wasn't in the cards at the time. However, Heaven always plays with a full deck.

Thus, began a deeper journey of utter dependence on my Father than I had ever known. Could I have been healed instantly? Absolutely. However, for me, the entire journey would be a miracle.

You see, dear friends, sometimes, our process is a miracle unfolding. That was my experience, a journey of miracles, scattered along my path like big jewels, one as beautiful, stunning, profound, and unique as the next. I would be awed by what God would do and as I was still reeling from that experience, I'd stumble upon another, miraculous jewel. On and on it went, continuing to "find a pleasant pool where others only find pain . . . " Along this jewel-laden path, I found this bedrock passage of Scripture to become my always.

How enriched are they who find their strength in the Lord; within their hearts are the highways of holiness! Even when their paths wind through the dark valley of tears, they dig deep to find a pleasant pool where others find only pain. He gives to them a brook of blessing filled from the rain of an outpouring.

They grow stronger and stronger with every step forward, and the God of all gods will appear before them in Zion.

- Psalm 84:5-7 (TPT)

The Conversation In Heaven

8
Build Me An Altar

As I mentioned earlier, I grew up with four sisters and one brother, me being the middle child. I have two sisters (fraternal twins) younger than me by only eighteen months. One of them, Dawn, and I, were particularly close growing up. We look very much alike and always enjoyed similar things. I must say, the combination of me as pitcher and Dawn at short stop on a softball field, made us unstoppable.

We shared everything together and rarely tired of each other. We used to push each other into random boys at the mall, wildly hoping to embarrass the other, ensuring all cool points would be lost. Sometimes, late at night, we'd sneak in each other's rooms, laughing our heads off, when we should have been sleeping for school the next day.

Dawn and I enjoyed going on mission trips together, shared youth group, and sweated at the gym (where we goofed off more than we worked out). We even went to college together for a couple of years before I graduated. She was my Maid of Honor in my wedding and threw me the cutest, most special bachelorette party.

Early on, when my former husband and I were building a church, she lived with us. She used to rock River and Lily Grace to sleep at night, playing countless hours with them when they were toddlers. I had the privilege of discipling

Dawn in her walk with God, even baptizing her. She gave me the treasure of sweet sisterhood.

A few years later, to my surprise, she expressed interest in going into the Navy. I didn't really know what to think of it, but I secretly hoped it would be a passing interest. Well, her interest grew into a reality and I found myself, along with my Mom and step dad, saying goodbye as she stepped on a charter bus with an entire group of unknown people making the same choice. Staying as strong as I could until that bus pulled out, waving fiercely as long as I could see her waving back, I burst into tears as soon as the bus was out of sight. I was so sad she was gone, having no idea when I would see her again.

We were the kind of sisters who just got each other. We could be on a long car ride, playing music and singing to the top of our lungs, or ride for hours quietly, knowing that was just fine too. We were so relaxed around each other, a relationship that didn't feel like it required a lot of work to grow. We had our sister disagreements like most, but made up quickly, not wanting to be disconnected for long at all.

Dawn would call me from wherever her ship was and I would respond as often as I could. With River and Lily only eighteen months apart and so young at the time, coupled with the church being in our home, busy was an understatement. Looking back, I wish I would have taken more time for her phone calls. She would call me with random cooking questions and we would end up pouring our hearts out to each other.

I remember feeling so sorry for all those boys in the Navy because Dawn was show-stopping gorgeous, long legs and a great personality to match. She was always thinking of others, always thinking of how she could gather people together and make them feel special. After her faithful and often lonely years on the ship, she finally got stationed in Naples, Italy. She was so excited for her own, cute, little place. She always had style, decorating her home like something out of a magazine.

Her first Thanksgiving there, she decided to host some Navy buddies over to her new place for a special holiday meal. I laughed when I found out she was doing this because she would tell you herself, she cannot cook. She would definitely look good doing it, but her specialty was coffee. That's about it. We had a good, informative conversation about menu ideas, recipes, and how to prepare a turkey. I about fell out of my chair, laughing when she called me after the party, telling me she didn't know to look inside the turkey before she cooked it to remove the white plastic bag, containing all its undesirable parts, so she cooked the turkey, leaving all that stuff inside!

During my third and what would be final separation with my husband, Dawn and I would have long, tear-filled conversations. I felt so heartbroken to share this news with her, knowing she looked up to me in so many areas, yet feeling I was failing her in this one. I knew it hurt her deeply. I think she looked at our marriage as hope for her dream to be married to come true one day too. When ours failed, I felt I had deeply let her down. She never said this, but I used to beat myself up about it for much longer than I ever should have, believing the lie that it was my responsibility to carry a perfect example of hope for her.

Often in life when we experience loss, hurt, or failure, we

will also experience the pain of letting others down. Our example and standard has and always will be Jesus, with our successes and failures finding their entire place in Him. There is also the truth that we will certainly miss the mark with ourselves and others in this life. That is just what sin is, missing the mark. When we can see our "miss" for what it is, grieve, repent and ask forgiveness whenever possible and equally important, forgive ourselves, the enemy's voice of accusation is strangled silent, never again able to hold us captive in regret.

Regret will cause you to believe the lie that you must live held captive in its grip to your failure, in a locked prison of blame, owing a false debt of penance that you feel shackled to pay. The truth is, there is no prison, no locked door and no shackles — the only ones that exist are the ones you allow in your mind. That debt and your freedom was paid for a long time ago by the only One who could write the check, unlock your chains and open the door.

Oh friend, the key is now in your hand. Unlock your own mind-created prison and set yourself free. As equally important, if you're struggling with unforgiveness, set that person free too. Read the following Scriptures over and over until you are free. There is no need to ask God to set you free from something He already has.

It's crucial we do this. By continuing to live in this false, unlocked, mind-made prison, we will not experience the freedom, then the confidence, then the assurance that our place of belonging is in the Face of God. We will remain camped out at His feet, begging for forgiveness. As beautiful as those Feet are, our loving Father, the great Lover of our soul, did not create us to live at His feet. The most intimate times shared between a husband and wife do not occur at the feet of their lover. True intimacy, the kind that can conceive, birth, and reproduce something eternal, must be lived in the Face of our Beloved.

Ponder these truths:

> *Whenever our hearts make us feel guilty and remind us of our failures, we know that God is much greater and more merciful than our conscience, and He knows everything there is to know about us. My delightfully loved friends, when our hearts don't condemn us, we have a bold freedom to speak face-to-face with God.*
>
> — 1 John 3:20-21 (TPT)

> *Now, there is no comparison between Adam's transgression and the gracious gift that we experience. For the magnitude of the gift far outweighs the crime. It's true that many died because of one man's transgression, but how much greater will God's grace and his gracious gift of acceptance overflow to many because of what one Man, Jesus, the Messiah, did for us! And this free-flowing gift imparts to us much more than what was given to us through the one who sinned. For because of one transgression, we are all facing a death sentence with a verdict of "Guilty!" But this gracious gift leaves us free from our many failures and brings us into the perfect righteousness of God— acquitted with the words "Not guilty!"*
>
> — Romans 5:15-16 (TPT)

> *And if anyone longs to be wise, ask God for wisdom and He will give it! He won't see your lack of wisdom as an opportunity to scold you over your failures, but He will*

overwhelm your failures with His generous grace.
- James 1:5 (TPT)

Gaze upon Him, join your life with His and joy will come. Your faces will glisten with glory. You'll never wear that shame-face again. - Psalm 34:5 (TPT)

I love this hymn we used to sing growing up:

> *Jesus paid it all*
> *All to Him I owe.*
> *Sin had left a crimson stain,*
> *He washed it white as snow.*
> *- "Jesus Paid It All," Kristian Stanfill*

Free yourself to live your life as white as snow, never to sling the mud of accusation on yourself or another and never allow the voice of accusation to be heard in the land of your mind and heart again.

One morning after I took the kids to school, I stopped by my Mom's for our usual coffee on the porch and prayer time. When I walked in the door, the look on her face told me something was very, very wrong. Two Navy men, dressed in full uniform, had knocked on the door, informing her that Dawn had been in a car accident on the way to the Navy base. During a very bad rainstorm, her car hydroplaned and she was killed on impact. I laid on my mom's kitchen floor, frozen in disbelief. This news, combined with my upcoming divorce battle, was unbelievably heartbreaking.

The grace and strength of the Lord carried me as I and my

sisters helped my Mom plan for the worst, the burial of her own daughter, our much-loved sister and my personal, life-long, best friend.

The weeks that followed seemed like a blur. Due to her death taking place in the Navy and the extent of the damage, the coroner and the entire process, took weeks. The Navy had their own service we were only able to watch online. Her funeral was postponed twice until they finally flew her over to us. Going through her things in my mom's garage was one of the most painful experiences I have endured. I drove around my mom's neighborhood for over thirty minutes before turning in, trying to muster up the strength to do it. I just stared at my sweet Dawn's, favorite coffee mug, still stained with her lipstick.

The church was packed. Navy personnel were there in full uniform. Dawn was given full, military honors. Unknown to any of us, just before her death, she was to be given the great honor of being chosen as "Sailor of the Year." Her commander gave her this award by pinning the medal on her beautiful, regal uniform as her body laid in the casket.

I had the great honor of delivering Dawn's eulogy. Quite honestly, the whole thing was surreal. Driving up to the Georgia National Cemetery, watching the military soldiers line up, play beautiful instruments, and shoot their powerful guns, was a fog. As one soldier folded the gorgeous flag of our country, knelt and gave it to my mom, I wasn't quite sure if I was still breathing.

The next week, I stepped into a divorce battle not to be wished on anyone. I remember knowing I had to put the deepest part of my grief of Dawn's death on the back burner of my heart while I was forced into this front burner divorce battle that must be fought.

A year later, the kids and I moved to where we are now and began to integrate our lives into the great life we now enjoy with our church family, our wonderful homeschool community and the lovely town we enjoy so much. However, just a year into it, we were still in the beginning stages of meeting people and creating new relationships. Having co-pastored the same church with the same people for twelve years, birthing babies and doing life together, starting over was difficult and at times, lonely and scary.

I was just getting to know the homeschool moms here who had already been enjoying years of friendship and life together. It was like looking in the rear-view mirror of my own, former life, where I too, had enjoyed rich relationships with women who had become my dear friends, sisters, if you will, some who were even present at the birth of my son, River. In the loss of my precious sister Dawn, combined with the loss of those friendships I had enjoyed so much for many years earlier, I now felt like the outsider, wondering if future, meaningful friendships would ever be restored.

As I was making the often difficult and insecure effort to build new relationships here, the anniversary of Dawn's death was approaching. Now that the divorce was finally over, I was slowly, layer by layer, starting to face the reality that my sister, my best friend, was gone. While everyone is certainly free to grieve in the way that seems best for them, I'm not one to frequently visit the grave of a loved one. I hadn't been to Dawn's grave since the funeral, yet I began to feel a growing desire to go. As I thought more about this, I felt the nearness of Heaven and then, an invitation, "Build Me an altar."

"What? You want me to build You an altar, Lord?"

As I pondered this further, I slowly began to understand what He was inviting me to do. Altars in the Bible were built for many different reasons, most often as sacred places for sacrifices and gifts to be offered up to God. Abraham built an altar to sacrifice his most loved son, Isaac. Noah built an altar to thank God for His covenant to never flood the earth again and the altar of incense in the tabernacle was used for the prayers of God's people to go up as sweet fragrances to the heavens. Clearly, the Altar where the ultimate Sacrifice was made, was the beautiful Cross.

I felt He wanted me to build an altar of thanksgiving for what He would do, an altar of hope for the future, at Dawn's grave. This was during the same season I wrote about earlier where the ugly, robber of a bulldozer was the predominant landscape fixture in my life. Yes, in the midst of very real grief and loss of one of the most precious gifts I've cherished most of my life, my much-loved Dawn, even at this time, where I could see no evidence of hope, Heaven was inviting me to build an altar into hope. While grief is most definitely a beautiful and very necessary thing, the Bible talks about grieving, with hope always in the room. This is very unnatural to the world's definition of grief, where hopelessness can wreak havoc.

Beloved brothers and sisters, we want you to be quite certain about the truth concerning those who have passed away, so that you won't be overwhelmed with grief like many others who have no hope. For if we believe that Jesus died and rose again, we also believe that God will bring with Jesus those who died while believing in Him. - 1 Thessalonians 4:13-14 (TPT)

Through Heaven's lens, we can take the hand of necessary grief and mourning, yet with the other hand grab hope in the midst of that grief and sorrow. For me, I knew Dawn had joined all of Heaven in extending the comfort-laden hand of hope for me to hold, choosing to believe I would enjoy rich, laughter-filled relationships with trusted, safe women again and that sisterhood would be restored; something that had been unjustly ripped from my life, along with my marriage, church, and community.

Our intentionally kind Father was inviting me in to something so beautiful, into a place of vulnerability, offering me an invitation to plant that vulnerability and process my grief with this new group of women I didn't even know very well yet.

He's such a loving Heavenly Father. He's the forever great and wise Gardener, looking for places to plant new growth in soil where all seems lost. He knew my deep desire for friendships I deeply enjoyed earlier in my life, friendships and even sisterhood like I had enjoyed with Dawn, my sorority sisters and other women in my life. In my beginning stages of grief over Dawn, Heaven was coming alongside me, placing a bag of seed in my hand, originating from the greenhouse of Heaven, taken from the luscious, enormous, life-filled, ever vibrant-colored plant, called hope.

Heaven never places a period on death. Jesus Himself conquered it, saying, *"Don't yield to fear. I am the*

Beginning and I am the End, the Living One! I was dead, but now look—I am alive forever and ever. And I hold the keys that unlock death and the unseen world" - Revelation 1:17b-18 (TPT).

I awkwardly and vulnerably invited every woman I desired deeper connection and relationship with to take an hour and a half road trip with me to visit my sisters' grave, having no idea if they would understand or even accept this strange invitation. To my relief and delight, almost every single one accepted.

It was a glorious trip as we wept and laughed together; my new friends so kindly and generously bundling up in the cold wind for a generous amount of time, kneeling together as we commemorated the beautiful life of cherished Dawn. My dear friend, Martha, even brought lovely wild flower seeds to plant at her grave.

Over three years later, as I look back, almost every single woman that was there, building that exquisite, yet painful altar with me, has become part of the dearest group of friends I have ever known—standing with me through a life-threatening cancer diagnosis, helping to clean my house, fold laundry, make meals and care for my children during my recovery, yet also letting me fully into their lives, enjoying church life together, discussing countless weight loss endeavors, crying and sharing each other's heartaches and triumphs, endlessly laughing, raising our kids and growing in God together, praising our hearts out in worship, taking vacations together and so much more.

Death is swallowed up by a triumphant victory! So

death, tell me, where is your victory? Tell me death, where is your sting? But we thank God for giving us the victory as conquerors through our Lord Jesus, the Anointed One. So now, beloved ones, stand firm and secure. Live your lives with an unshakable confidence. We know that we prosper and excel in every season by serving the Lord because we are assured that our union with the Lord makes our labor productive with fruit that endures. - 1 Corinthians 15:55, 57-58 (TPT)

Oh dear friend, anytime we experience the loss of a loved one, when death stares your heart in the face, mocking that it has had the final word, I can guarantee that from Heaven's lens where there is a tomb, there is a womb. Jesus passed through a tomb to bring us out through Heaven's womb into resurrected new life.

So, if you've experienced death or loss, grieve, dear one, and rest assured, knowing a womb, the birthing of something new, will reveal itself in time.

If you are standing at what seems to be a dead end, a Red Sea is looking to be parted. If you are experiencing loss of any kind, a gain is on the horizon. The laws of Heaven are just waiting to be governed and implemented by us, inviting us to take Hope in one hand and comfort in the other as we join the stride of Heaven, stepping as citizens into our inherited, rightful and eternal land of the Kingdom in which we belong, the land of righteousness, peace and joy.

9
Surround Yourself with People Who Can See Your Army

During my recovery from a full mastectomy, I remember feeling so grateful for how well we were taken care of. Having no family close, this was pretty amazing. Our incredible church family, my college sorority sisters, my gym community where I taught classes, the kids' homeschool organization, and many more, rallied around us. My children even set up a petting zoo as a fundraiser for our town which was a great success. I was blown away. My kids were blown away.

That Christmas, I was out of work, healing. We ended up having the best Christmas ever. There were so many gifts under the Christmas tree, it was hard to keep track of them all. I remember laying so many generous gift cards out on the coffee table, they ended up covering the entire table! The kids and I just knelt there, thanking God for His faithfulness and goodness.

As I laid in bed, healing, drains hanging out of parts they shouldn't, I felt so comforted by all of Heaven. I felt safe, known, and loved. People from church would come over around the clock, bringing us meals or just to visit. While it may sound wild, most of my memories during that recovery time included laughter and lots of Snapchats. My dear girlfriends would come over and take turns cleaning, cooking, and caring for the animals. This was a hilarious scene because most of my girlfriends do not enjoy animals. At one point, my dear friend, Meredith, had to sprint down the street to recover our runaway donkey, Levi.

I learned something valuable in this season. I learned to surround myself with friends who could see my "army." There is a story told in 2 Kings 6:11-17, where the King of Aram was frustrated and angry at the prophet, Elisha. Through Elisha's prophetic insight, he would tell Israel, the king of Aram's plan of attack, allowing them to dodge the Aramean army every time. Whether you believe in prophecy or not, having prophets in your life can really come in handy. When the world's counterfeits are fortune tellers, etc., God's insight shared with a human being for your benefit is one of the coolest things to experience. You also can share in this gift because Revelation 19:10 tells us the very *"testimony of Jesus is the spirit of prophecy"* (TPT). If Jesus lives inside of you, you can prophesy. Here is how the story of Elisha and the Aramean army unfolds:

> *When the king of Aram was at war with Israel, he would confer with his officers and say, "We will mobilize our forces at such and such a place." But immediately Elisha, the man of God, would warn the king of Israel, "Do not go near that place, for the Arameans are planning to mobilize their troops there."*
>
> *So the king of Israel would send word to the place indicated by the man of God. Time and again Elisha warned the king, so that he would be on the alert there. The king of Aram became very upset over this. He called his officers together and demanded, "Which of you is*

the traitor? Who has been informing the king of Israel of my plans?" "It's not us, my lord the king," one of the officers replied. "Elisha, the prophet in Israel, tells the king of Israel even the words you speak in the privacy of your bedroom!"

"Go and find out where he is," the king commanded, "so I can send troops to seize him." And the report came back: "Elisha is at Dothan."

So one night the king of Aram sent a great army with many chariots and horses to surround the city. When the servant of the man of God got up early the next morning and went outside, there were troops, horses, and chariots everywhere. "Oh sir, what will we do now?" the young man cried to Elisha. "Don't be afraid!" Elisha told him. "For there are more on our side than on theirs!" Then Elisha prayed, "O Lord, open his eyes and let him see!" The Lord opened the young man's eyes, and when he looked up, he saw that the hillside around Elisha was filled with horses and chariots of fire.

- 2 Kings 6:8-16 (NLT)

It's very important in your life, especially when you face difficult things, that you strategically surround yourself with those who can see your army, your horses and chariots of fire. I felt it was very important not to YouTube everything about this cancer, hear stories of others that provoked fear or allow people in my life who were not filled with hope for me during this time, even if I was related to them.

This may sound harsh, but it wasn't. I was loving me well by doing this. I learned something in counseling from one of my mentors, Wendy Backlund. She says, "Never counsel anyone you don't have hope for." This is so true. The same is true when you seem to be in a hopeless situation. Heaven is never experiencing a shortage of hope, so you reserve the right to surround yourself with those in your life who are echoing Heaven's voice of hope over you, encouraging you to do the same.

Give yourself full permission to be picky in those you allow to have a voice in your life, especially in times of crisis. If the sound coming out of their mouth isn't lining up with life, hope, and peace, create healthy and loving boundaries around you so you are able to keep your eyes on the army full of horses and chariots of fire surrounding you, the army that is so much more for you than against you.

Caring people and friends would lovingly bring me all kinds of herbs, oils, articles, mail me books and much more. I even remember trying to juice what seemed like a hundred ingredients to ensure my body would be cancer free. While I was so grateful for their love and care, I found myself beginning to feel overwhelmed, knowing I couldn't financially keep up with all the different regimens, and if I tried, I would have spent most of the day living in the kitchen or the bathroom. Homeschool teaching would have been difficult from either of those places.

Feeling overwhelmed by all this brought with it fear and anxiety, like I was depending on my own efforts to heal myself, grasping at everything that sounded good. That's exactly what it was, grasping, and grasping involves desperation. Heaven is never in a desperate place and neither should we be.

When I began to feel that way, peace seemed to vanish, and fear would creep in. This is when I knew to back up, quiet my soul and find peace again.

For me, my peace rested in the truth that I had to fling myself upon the all sufficiency of Jesus to be my Healer. I knew I was utterly and completely dependent upon Him and this became my land of peace. Oh friends, I have learned Peace to be the GPS of Heaven and our hearts.

> *You will keep him in perfect peace, whose mind is stayed on You because he trusts in You.* - Isaiah 26:3 (NLT).

If our mind is kept on Him and His Word, we are guaranteed to experience perfect peace. What a gift we can give to this world since we live in a time where everywhere you turn, it seems another anti-anxiety medication is put on the market. Perfect peace is always available, and the key lies with us and our decision to keep our thoughts on Him. We will have no problem trusting Him when He has been given full residency in our minds and hearts.

Matthew 5:9 says, *"Blessed are the peacemakers, for it is they who will be recognized as sons of God"* (WNT). Said another way, one of the primary ways you can recognize a son or daughter of God is by the peace they carry. How recognizable are you, dear friend?

There were certainly healthy steps I took and a few books I read but only if they kept me in the land of peace, life and hope. If I started to read or watch something and it brought fear or desperation with it, I would quickly put it down, fighting to guard and keep my peace. Some would call that denial. I call it wisdom and warfare, just packaged a little differently.

The Conversation In Heaven

10
Jesus Likes Watching the Olympics

So, what did I do at that time? I remember feeling like Heaven wanted me to tune into the 2016 Olympics. Doesn't that sound strange? Sometimes, while I was being "holy" and reading my Bible or earnestly praying, I would feel strongly that I should watch the Olympics. Finally, I asked the Lord about this and He said, "I want you to watch the Olympics; watch how champions train and win because you are a champion."

One Olympian was highlighted to me above the rest. It was Kristin Armstrong, the USA cyclist. She won her first gold medal in Beijing in 2008, at thirty-five years old. She then decided to retire and have a family. She gave birth to a son. When he was two, she said she kept having a vision of him on the podium with her as she received another gold medal. That vision became reality when she came out of retirement and reclaimed her second gold medal in London in 2012, with her two-year-old son on her hip, as she stood on the podium! Astoundingly, Kristin was back again for the Olympic games in Rio in 2016, the oldest woman on the team by seven years. When asked why she would take the risk of coming back, she answered, "Because I can."

I watched in awe as this forty-two-year-old woman, (one year older than me at the time), on the eve of her forty-third birthday, after winning two consecutive gold medals for cycling, won her third consecutive gold medal! As soon as she knew she had won, she fell to the ground, laying on her side with a throbbing hip and bleeding nose. In an interview that very same day, Kristin said, "I've learned over the years that the focus is not on the outside. It's not about me being over forty. People ask me how I did it and I tell them it's everything between your ears. It's your mindset. Keep positive, believe in yourself and surround yourself with people who believe in you."

I was deeply encouraged as I watched, with my own eyes, this incredible woman do what was thought to be impossible. All of Heaven and my wonderful Jesus was watching the Olympics that day, telling me I was just as much a champion as Kristin. I certainly didn't feel like a champion, being at my weakest point, two very important and extremely feminine parts of my body removed, not able to work and certainly not my usual picture of health or fitness to anyone around me. However, the hope that was infused in my soul that day was like a permanent inoculation against fear that has immunized me to this very day.

Oh friends, we must tune in to what Heaven is saying over us. I can assure you, it will always be drenched in hope, no matter your present circumstance. You, too, are a champion and Heaven will never change Its conversation on the truth about you. What about the conversation going on between your ears? Do you have hope for *you?*

Graham Cooke says, "The real battle in the world is with hope. Hope is the favorable and confident expectation of goodness." God is forever and always a God of goodness.

Ask yourself if there is any part of you that is not believing this vital truth. Your belief in this truth is linked to your expectation of Him to be good, to you. Oh champion-friend, you too have a tailor-made, gold medal forever hanging around your neck and a podium to rightfully stand on as a champion because of everything Jesus did and is. You *are* because He *is*. Live your entire life permanently on that podium—in your mind, in your heart. When you inhale and exhale, you are that champion. Anything or anyone that would say different is under the influence of a lie.

The Conversation In Heaven

11
Be Sure and Bring a Basket to Your Valley

As I mentioned earlier, I have been a fitness professional for a long time. After my first surgery, involving a full mastectomy, as I spent time at home recovering, drains so stylishly hanging from body parts now gone, it was hard to imagine I would be able to exercise again any time soon. I missed my daily workout routines. I have always found enjoyment in exercise. At times, it has served me well as my own form of therapy.

I have exercised on a rebounder (a mini-trampoline), for years and have always loved my big backyard trampoline as well. I used it as my secret sauce for previous beauty pageant swimsuit victories, as part of my normal, fitness routine and just for plain fun. One winter, I shoveled snow off of the one in my backyard, just so I wouldn't miss my jumping time.

As I recovered, my rebounder now sat in the corner of my living room, housing my laundry. I would look at it from time to time, longing for the day I could jump again. As I was healing, when I would start to pray and meditate on God, something very strange would happen. I would be so drawn to that rebounder! Knowing I most certainly couldn't jump at the time, I kept wondering why I couldn't seem to stop thinking about it, almost like it was calling to me. I know that sounds strange but look at this peculiar truth found in Isaiah 45:3, *"I will give you the treasures of darkness and hidden wealth of secret places, so that you may know that it is I, The LORD, the God of Israel, who calls you by your name"* (ESV).

When we go through dark times of many kinds— becoming ill, losing a job, enduring deep heartbreak, or bad news delivered right to the front door of our hearts—I have discovered something profoundly amazing. In the difficulties this life brings, Heaven always has treasures, hidden riches to be found, opportunities for upgrades, all around.

These upgrades are available in our thinking, through doors into greater things, leaps and bounds in growth, gifts of ideas the world needs that just may house our provision, wrapped and waiting to be discovered, content to be hidden, knowing they will be found in our darkest hour. I like to think of it like some sort of Divine Easter egg hunt, all hidden within the valleys of our life.

It's wild how the Kingdom of God works. The Israelites, God's people, after being in bondage to the Egyptians for hundreds of years, are finally led out to freedom, only to follow God's path, led by Moses, right up to what completely looked and was, a dead end, a huge sea, a watery grave, insolently staring them in the face. They had no idea that dark, difficult and impossible place would be Heaven's doorway into their longed-for promised land. Indeed, their pathway of hidden treasure also became the watery grave that would forever silence the enemy that had held them and their destiny captive for so long.

Another favorite example of the mind-blowing operations of Heaven is found with one of my favorite Old Testament kings, King Jehoshaphat. He is told some terrible news that a huge army, comprised of many of Israel's enemies, had all combined forces to attack Judah. They were coming to drive out God's people from the land that was already their inheritance, the land meant for them to completely occupy and enjoy.

King Jehoshaphat knew he was outnumbered. The Bible says in 2 Chronicles 20:3, *"In mounting fear, Jehoshaphat devoted himself to seek the Lord"* (NLT). I love the heart of this king. He didn't even waste time developing his own "try" because he knew he was staring "impossible" in the face. He knew he had to fling his entire trust and dependency into the ability of his victorious God, not in his own striving efforts.

> *O our God, won't you stop them? We are powerless against this mighty army that is about to attack us. We do not know what to do, but we are looking to You for help . . . our eyes are on You.*
>
> *- 2 Chronicles 20:12 (NLT)*

In verses 15 through 17, God answers his honest cry and speaks through a man named Jahaziel.

> *Stop being afraid, and stop being discouraged because of this vast invasion force, because the battle doesn't belong to you, but to God. You'll find them at the end of the valley. . . You won't be fighting in this battle. Stand still, watch the LORD's salvation on your behalf! Never fear and never be discouraged. Go out to face them tomorrow, since the LORD is with you (NLT).*

King Jehoshaphat appointed singers to walk ahead of the army, singing to the Lord and praising Him for His holy splendor. This is what they sang: "Give thanks to the LORD; His faithful love endures forever!" At the very moment they began to sing and give praise, the Lord caused the enemy armies to start fighting among themselves.

When the army of Judah arrived at the lookout point in the wilderness, all they saw were dead bodies lying on the ground as far as they could see. Not a single enemy had escaped (ESV).

God's people spent three days collecting the abandoned equipment, clothing, and valuables because there was so much. Before leaving, they gathered together and praised God, naming that valley "The Valley of Beracah," which means blessing.

Oh friends, did you catch that? *Beracah* means blessing! Even when you walk through the valley, enemies lurking, make sure you carry a big basket, big enough to hold the hidden blessings and treasures that can only be found there, just waiting for you to gather.

I finally asked the Lord, "What are you trying to say about the rebounder?" I felt He wanted me to research about rebound exercise, what it does to the body. Now, I have been jumping for years, thinking it was my secret thing, a fun way to help keep me in shape. What a strange urging

I sensed from Him to research what rebounding actually does for the body, yet my curiosity won out.

As I began to research, I was completely blown away. I

couldn't believe my findings. I discovered that rebound exercise has been around for years and years, written about in medical journals as the "cancer answer." I found statements like, "never be sick again by jumping." I even found a quote from NASA, (National Aeronautics and Space Administration) that said, "Rebound exercise is the most effective exercise yet devised by man."

Further study revealed countless sources saying it is the best way to cleanse our crucial lymphatic system (the body's dumping post for disease). Our lymph system runs linear and has no pump of its own, being totally dependent on physical exercise to move. The Creator has brilliantly designed it this way because as humans, our bodies have a built-in need for movement. Without it, our cells are left stewing in their own waste products and starving for nutrients, a situation that contributes to arthritis, cancer, infection and other degenerative diseases. Exercise alone helps get our lymphatic system going but by utilizing the huge benefits of gravity and the vertical motion of rebounding, we create a pumping action that helps our lymph system to cleanse our body of toxins, infection and disease much more efficiently and effectively than any other form of horizontal motion exercise, like jogging, running or cycling.

Another game-changing benefit of rebounding is the utilization of gravity. All cells in the body become stronger in response to the increased G-force during rebounding, and this cellular exercise results in our self-propelled immune cells being up to five times more active. Since these cells make it their job to eat viruses, bacteria, and even cancer cells, rebound exercise directly strengthens the immune system.

Rebounding is gentle on the joints, with no solid ground to suddenly stop the bouncing of your feet, abruptly jarring our bones and joints like pavement does. It reduces your body fat, firms your legs, thighs, stomach, arms, and hips, increases your agility, and improves your sense of balance. Rebound exercise strengthens your muscles overall, provides an aerobic effect for your heart, rejuvenates your body when it's tired, and generally puts you in a great state of health and fitness.

So, what was just one of the many, many treasures I gathered in my basket from the valley? A dream come true for me— my own, fitness rebounding company that is now helping so many, called Jumpology. Jumpology was a treasure, hidden and waiting for me to discover, in the darkness of my valley. As the enemy stood in that valley, waiting to destroy, not only was he entirely defeated, Heaven had hidden "plunder and valuables" in that valley of blessing, that I have most definitely spent more than three days gathering. Gathering not just for me but for many others. That's how the Kingdom works, my friends. Our victories are exponential, benefitting all those around us.

You too, have others waiting on the other side of your valley, waiting for you to come out, loaded down with baskets and baskets of blessings; blessings that will be spilling over with so much freedom, hope and healing, for the nations. These blessings are tailored made for you, only to be found by you; releasing a freedom and joy that will continually nourish your very soul and many others— others you may never meet, others who will read your story and be profoundly impacted by your choices.

12
When Fear Comes Knocking, Answer the Door!

You may be reading this, finding it hard to believe that I could go through something like this as if I went skipping down a path of gumdrops. No, no, not true. I definitely had some very hard and scary moments, moments like the Grim Reaper himself was standing in my bedroom. Yet I learned something significant when those times would come.

The Holy Spirit taught me something about fear. Fear is a spirit. None of us were born with fear. It's something sent from our enemy. . . a spirit. 2 Timothy 1:7 says, *"For God will never give you the spirit of fear, but the Holy Spirit Who gives you mighty power, love, and a sound mind"* (TPT).

I remember one night having a hard time sleeping, being tormented with fearful thoughts about this cancer diagnosis and what it might mean. My mind played out scenes of my kids growing up without me, flashes of my funeral and so much more, trying to suffocate me. I sat straight up in bed and felt the spirit of fear in my room. Then I heard the Lord say to me, "When fear comes knocking, answer the door."

Now, this may seem strange but it's just as strange as a burglar being at your door, banging, wanting you to let him in. Would you just sit there and let him keep banging on the door, tormenting and bullying everyone in your home with fear of danger? No! You would call the police and possibly take matters into your own hands.

Well, it's a very similar situation with the spirit of fear. You see, the Bible tells us that fear involves torment. Our Father doesn't want us to ever experience torment. So, He was telling me to answer the door and tell fear to leave. Remember, dear friends, fear never has to have a place in your life, only the one you give it. My mentor used to say, "The devil may be the prince and power of the air but not the air I breathe." He was exactly right.

Picture your heart and mind so filled with the wonderful Person of Jesus and all the fruit of the Spirit that there is nowhere fear can sit. All of Heaven and Its Fruit, bountifully expressed by love, growing in full maturity in your life are occupying and enjoying every "chair" and piece of furniture within your heart.

See love, entirely reclining back in the Lazy Boy of your heart; joy, swingin' on the front porch of your soul, peace, sitting at the desk of your mind, patience, chillin' out on your couch, kindness, sipping a cup of tea at your heart's kitchen table, goodness, contentedly sitting by the living room fireplace, faithfulness, happily vacuuming; gentleness, propped up on a pillow, reading a book and self-control, doing an exercise video in front of your TV.

Friends, in light of this scene, fear has got to go! So, when fear comes knocking on the door of your heart and mind, answer the door with all the truth of Heaven and watch it flee, coat-tails flying in the wind. You see, faith has its finest hour in the midst of fear, not apart from it.

The Bible says that an obnoxious giant named Goliath ran his ugly mouth for forty days and nights, taunting and torturing the people of God, keeping them frozen with fear. The more his bullying voice was given a stage to be heard, the more the spirit of fear grew within their hearts. David looked that giant of fear and intimidation called Goliath right in the face and was angry his voice had been heard so long in the land of his people. You see, because fear had been given a voice, the spirit of fear had breeding ground to grow, thus shutting down the courage, confidence and faith of God's people. The voice of fear must always be silenced. No voice, no stage, no spirit, and certainly no defeat, plain and simple.

David had enough. He ran toward that ugly giant, killed him with a small stone and used Goliath's own sword to cut off his head. David's brothers, King Saul and even Goliath, had made mocking comments earlier about David's small size and inexperience. However, the truth was, David had been killing giants of fear for quite some time before he encountered Goliath. Being an unassuming shepherd at the time, he knew God had been with him in killing a lion and a bear, to protect his sheep.

David's faith in his God was larger than any giant the Philistine army could create. In our own lives, fear always comes as a giant, with intimidation in its voice; always wanting to make us feel little, weak and powerless in its grasp. By answering the voice of the ugly spirit of fear with the voice of Truth, you silence and annihilate the sound that is being rehearsed and played in your land (your mind), thus giving no breeding ground for the spirit of fear to take root and grow.

Interestingly enough, the name Goliath means to "uncover or reveal." The voice of fear must be uncovered and revealed for what it is and then cut off by your voice of faith, echoing the sound of Heaven. It doesn't matter how outnumbered you or your situation may appear or feel, the remaining truth is, Heaven never has a shortage of power, so neither do you. Believe it and silence every voice of fear by answering the door with the truth of Heaven.

For me, when the Goliath called cancer tried to intimidate me through a man in a white coat with a diagnosis, I heard the voice of fear knocking; but then, I heard a greater Voice of Truth wanting me to answer the door.

After two painful biopsies in my lungs and then another, very painful biopsy of a lymph node in my clavicle, to my shock all came back positive. As I sat there in my oncologist's office, he looked at me and said, "This is what I feared. The cancer has learned to travel and is now in your lymph nodes. It is terminal, inoperable and you will die from this."

Struggling to take this information in, I felt the Goliath of fear taunting me. I gripped the back of my dear friend Rachel's sweatshirt as she lovingly and supportively stood next to me. I felt tears form in my eyes and then I heard the Voice of my wonderful Jesus ask me a question—no hesitation, worry or sympathy in His sound—just beautiful, bold, fiery love and firmness, "But Who do you say that I am?" He asked His disciples this same question:

When Jesus came to Caesarea Philippi, He asked His disciples this question: "What are the people saying about Me, the Son of Man? Who do they believe I am?" They answered, "Some are convinced You are John the Baptizer, others say You are Elijah reincarnated, or Jeremiah, or one of the prophets."

But you—who do you say that I am?" Jesus asked. Simon Peter spoke up and said, "You are the Christ, the Anointed One, the Son of the living God!" Jesus replied, "You are favored and privileged Simon, son of Jonah! For you didn't discover this on your own, but my Father in Heaven has supernaturally revealed it to you...this truth of Who I am will be the bedrock foundation on which I will build My church—and the power of death will not be able to overpower it! I will give you the keys of Heaven's kingdom realm to forbid on earth that which is forbidden in Heaven, and to release on earth that which is released in Heaven."

- Matthew 16:13-19 (TPT)

You see, friends, Jesus was lovingly asking me to stand on the truth of Who He was and is, inside my body, of Who He is inside your body, inside of all His sons and daughters. We have the keys to forbid here on this earth what is forbidden in Heaven and I can tell you, every cancer and all disease is most definitely forbidden in Heaven.

There is no truth that any disease is given to teach us a lesson or any truth in the statement, "If it's God's will to heal me, then He will." There was no "if" on every excruciating and Oh so costly, stripe our Jesus took on His Back for the complete healing of all mankind.

How can God give anyone a disease when it is not found in Heaven? When it is certainly not found in Him? Healing is Who He is. His will must always line up with His nature. His very nature is to heal. The truth of Who He is inside of our earth as well as the earth is what we are able to release inside ourselves and in all those around us. The truth of Who He is within us is how He is building His church.

I sat on that table, in my oncologist's office, instantly feeling relieved and strengthened by the question Jesus asked me, knowing He and all of Heaven had rushed in to rescue me with eternal truth. Quite frankly, I could sense His disdain at this bully of fear, trying to mess with His daughter. Straightening up, tears leaving my eyes, I heard myself answer Him back in my heart, "This is going to be a great line in my book." And indeed, it is.

Oh yes, friends, fear will come knocking, and the best news is you are free and empowered to answer the door, with all of Heaven at your back!

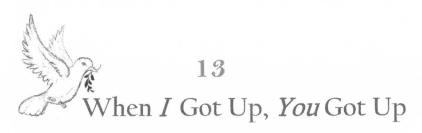

13
When *I* Got Up, *You* Got Up

After the conversation in my oncologist's office, where I was told the cancer had come back in my lungs, clavicle and lymph nodes and that it was terminal and inoperable, I took a little trip out of the country to see a friend. My friend was also a doctor who had helped many with cancer, but I could tell even she was rattled by this diagnosis and the PET scan findings.

One late night while I was there, I determined to meet with God about this. I was struggling with some fear, desperate to know what He had to say. Everyone was asleep. I sat out by the pool and felt the nearness of Heaven. I sensed His Presence close in. I began to pace by the pool and seemed to revert to my old self (fear will often lead you backward).

I tried to recall anyone and everyone I might not have forgiven, any sin of the past that could be blocking my healing or may have caused this cancer to come back, making the huge mistake of believing the lie that His ability to heal was about me. I went through the laundry list in my mind, asking Him about each person and situation, painfully playing memories over and over, like a miserable, punishing movie reel.

I just sensed Him waiting there, waiting until I was done torturing myself. As I carried on, He just waited, with no comments about any of them, like He had no idea what I was talking about, yet I could sense He wanted me to be "done" because He had something entirely different He'd like to discuss. Stubbornly, I continued asking Him to bring up any face of any person I needed to forgive until He finally said, "Abigail, I don't want to talk to you about any of that. I took care of that a long time ago, but you haven't. Perhaps the face you most need to see is yours. Forgive you, Abigail. Forgive *you*."

I was undone. I thought I had forgiven myself, but shame and guilt still had a presence in my heart. I wept in gratitude as I forgave myself and allowed any and every scene of my life that still felt painful, to fully emerge. I sat right down in each memory, applied His beautiful Blood to it, and moved on. When I was done, He was still there, just lovingly and patiently waiting for me to finish. He took no ownership of the chains of guilt and shame I had around me, yet He was entirely there, fully believing in me as my Champion Friend, to free myself and fully embrace the freedom He had already won for me a long time ago. He knew there was nothing more for Him to do, so that's why He patiently waited, waited for me to free myself, take hold of everything He had already done for me and make it my own.

It was so enlightening and empowering. I felt so loved by Him, so believed in by My Father. With this empowering kind of faith, no wonder He says if we just had a tiny mustard seed of it, we could move mountains.

When I was done, I knew He wanted to take a walk with me.

This part was like an open vision, one where I fully knew where I was and my surroundings, yet I was also very aware of Him and where I was in the Spirit. We walked on terrain back in historical, Biblical time. This was very easy for me to embrace because I was part of a study tour to Israel while in college.

We walked up to the cross. I saw Him hanging there, yet He was standing next to me as well. He said, "Abigail, you have always done well at receiving My Blood in your life but there is more."

We walked on, past the cross, to the opening of the tomb. As we walked inside, I saw Him lying there, yet again, He was standing next to me.

He asked me, "Do you see Me laying there?"

I said, "Yes, Sir. Yes, I do."

He said, "Watch Me get up."

He then sat up on that slab of stone, inside the tomb. When He sat up, He looked at me and said, "Abigail, did you see Me get up?"

I said, "Yes, yes I did."

With such love and intention, a Fatherly intention wrapped in strength, one with fiery desire for truth He wanted me to take and make my own, He then said,

"Abigail, when *I* got up, *you* got up."

Oh friends, this penetrated me so deeply. It was like He unfolded the beautiful truth of Romans 8:11, one of my favorite verses, layer by layer, peeling back all the glorious truth found within.

> *Once the Spirit of Him who raised Jesus from the dead lives within you He will, by that same Spirit, bring to your whole being new strength and vitality* (NTME).

By that *same* Spirit. That means same measure, same fullness. The same measuring system of Heaven is ours, for the here and now. Notice He says He will bring to your "whole being, new strength and vitality." "Whole being" is translated your mortal, fleshly, physical body. Why would He want you to experience the fullness of His Spirit inside you anywhere else but here, on this earth?

He proved it by coming to this earth as our perfect Example. This is why He kept His gaze steadily on the Father and finished His assignment. He is our Forerunner, the Bible says, our Door into the life we can live too—His life. It's like He ran the race, crossed the finish line, turned around and said, "Come on! I did it, so you can too!"

We get to mirror from Heaven who and Whose we already are. This is how we are a sign and wonder to the world. This is how He wants others to see and receive His Kingdom. This is how we let His Kingdom come and His will be done, on this earth, your earth (pinch yourself as you read this, touch your mind, your heart, your eyes, your ears, your lips). It's you where He wants the fullness of Himself to be.

Paul says it best in 2 Corinthians 4:7, *"We are like common clay jars that carry this glorious treasure within, so that the extraordinary overflow of power will be seen as God's"* (TPT). The focus is never to be on our hang ups, inadequacies, or inconsistencies of the "common clay," the earth suit we walk around in. We can entirely rest ourselves on the glorious treasure within our clay.

We must first grasp this eternal truth for ourselves, then we are able to give it away to the world around us.

So here I am, standing in the tomb, continuing to have this beautiful conversation with my wonderful Jesus. After He asked me if I saw Him get up, He then swung His legs around and stood up. When He stood up, again, He looked at me and asked,

"Abigail, did you see Me stand up?"

I said, "I sure did."

He then said, "Abigail, when *I* stood up, *you* stood up."

He walked to the entrance of the tomb and as He stood in its opening, He looked at me over His shoulder and said, "I'm about to walk out of this tomb, Abigail. When *I* walked out, *you* walked out with Me. Abigail, was there cancer in *My* lungs when I walked out of the tomb?"

With my heart bursting in complete devotion to Him and unspeakable joy for what He was so lovingly showing me, I said, "No, Sir. There was no cancer in Your lungs."

He then asked me, "Does there have to be cancer in *your* lungs?"

I answered Him, "No. No, there does not."

He asked me, "Abigail, does *anyone* have to have cancer in their body?"

I said, "No, Jesus, no they do not."

He then asked, "Abigail, when I walked out of the tomb, was *I* depressed?"

I said, "No, Jesus, no You were not."

He lovingly asked, "Abigail, does *anyone* have to suffer from depression?"

I replied, "No, no they do not."

That was it. The vision ended. I just stood there, stunned in awe and wonder. A great awareness welled up inside me that I had been given Heaven's keys to this truth, keys attached to a key ring of holy responsibility to steward them well. This book is part of that stewardship.

As I stood there, a great and full assurance of my healing was realized. I knew in that moment my entire body was healed and cancer free. I returned home with a PET scan already on the calendar.

The morning of the scan, I woke up hearing the words, "This is the glory scan." How exciting! I was so worry-free about this scan that I scheduled a fun hike with my dear friend, Quin. I was more focused on the fun we would have on our hike than I was about that scan. During previous scans, I would take a loving friend for support. I felt no need this time, knowing my greatest Friend was right by my side. I hummed love songs to the Lord while I was in the scan tube and then skipped off for a fun hike with Quin.

That afternoon I waited in anticipation for a phone call. The nurse called while I was waiting in the homeschool carpool line to pick up River and Lily Grace. I sat there on the phone, with a smirk on my face,

"Yes? Well? What did you find?"

The nurse stumbled and fumbled over her words as she said, "Well, uh, there's nothing here.

The spots that were there before are gone and there is no activity in the lymph nodes."

I shouted in gratitude and joy for all of Heaven (and the carpool moms) to hear. Three months later, another scan revealed absolutely no activity anywhere, my oncologist stating that my lymph nodes were perfect. I asked him what he thought about all this and he said, "Well, it doesn't take my medical degree on the wall to see that this is a miracle."

I joined in with Heaven's celebration as streamers and party banners seemed to glisten all around. I was celebrating His wonderful faithfulness and goodness yet at the same time, I had this keen awareness that all of Heaven was also celebrating *me* and my choice to believe. Isn't that mind-blowing? We truly are surrounded by the great cloud of witnesses, constantly cheering us on to pursue and possess all that is ours, celebrating and believing in us to be victorious in that pursuit.

As for us, we have all of these great witnesses who encircle us like clouds. So, we must let go of every wound that has pierced us and the sin we so easily fall into. Then we will be able to run life's marathon race with passion and determination, for the path has been already marked out before us. We look away from the natural realm and we fasten our gaze onto Jesus Who birthed faith within us and Who leads us forward into faith's perfection. His example is this: Because His heart was focused on the joy of knowing that you would be His, He endured the agony of the cross and conquered its humiliation, and now sits exalted at the right hand of the throne of God! So, consider carefully how Jesus faced such intense opposition from sinners who opposed their own souls, so that you won't become worn down and cave in under life's pressures.

- Hebrews 12:1-3 (TPT)

What an amazing truth. He birthed faith *within* us. Have you ever gone through something difficult, yet felt a strength and faith rise up within you, only to be talked out of it by those around you who weren't choosing to access that same faith? Those who wanted you to "face reality?"

Friends, the lens of Heaven is our reality! We are invited to "look away from this natural realm" and focus on Jesus, the One who birthed faith within us—all the faith we will ever need in any given situation, with limitless access to it. Yet, when we take our gaze off of the Person of faith within, off of our Jesus, and focus on the circumstances without, it's very similar to Peter getting out of the boat to follow Jesus on the water. Peter walks toward Jesus steadily—until he looks at the waves. It is only when Peter's *gaze* changed that his *walk* changed.

Oh friends, my deepest prayer for you in reading this book, is that for all your days, you make the life-changing decision to fix your gaze through the lens of Heaven.

There is no wave high enough, no trouble big enough, no disease dark enough, and no pain deep enough for Heaven's conversation to ever be silenced on the eternal truth that your outcome has and always will be hope-filled victory!

Resources

To find out more about Abigail, book a speaking engagement or schedule a Hope Session (counseling sessions for individuals, couples and families), visit: girlofhope.com

To learn more about Bethel Atlanta Church or to find out about how you can enroll in BASSM (Bethel Atlanta School of Supernatural Ministry), please visit bethelatlanta.com

To learn more about Pastor Bill Johnson & Bethel Church in Redding, California, please visit bethelredding.com

To schedule a Sozo session for inner healing, anywhere in the world, visit Bethelsozo.com

To learn more about Dr. Christopher Saxon and natural ways to heal your body, please visit Saxonhealth.com

To learn more about Jumpology & rebound exercise, visit girlofhope.com or on:

Facebook at: www.facebook.com/jumpology.fit

Instagram as JumpologyFitness

To purchase the world's best rebounder, the Cellerciser, please visit my good friend, Dave Hall at Cellercise.com

Made in the USA
Columbia, SC
01 November 2019